THE PROBLEM OF STYLE

THE PROBLEM OF STYLE

J MIDDLETON MURRY

GREENWOOD PRESS, PUBLISHERS
WESTPORT, CONNECTICUT

Library of Congress Cataloging in Publication Data

Murry, John Middleton, 1889-1957.
  The problem of style.

  Reprint of the ed. published by Oxford
University Press, London, which was issued as
no. 11 of Oxford paperbacks.
    1. Style, Literary--Addresses, essays, lectures.
I. Title.
PN203.M8 1980   808   80-21463
ISBN 0-313-22523-0 (lib. bdg.)

First edition 1922; ninth impression 1956. This is a reprint of the
1976 impression of the first Oxford Paperbacks issue 1960.

This reprint has been authorized by the Oxford University Press.

Reprinted in 1980 by Greenwood Press
a division of Congressional Information Service, Inc.
88 Post Road West, Westport, Connecticut 06881

Printed in the United States of America

10 9 8 7 6 5 4 3 2 1

TO THE
PRINCIPAL, FELLOWS, AND SCHOLARS
OF BRASENOSE COLLEGE, OXFORD

PREFATORY NOTE

The six lectures reprinted in this volume were delivered in the school of English Literature at Oxford on the invitation of Sir Walter Raleigh, in the Summer Term of 1921. Where it was necessary to curtail them I have restored them to their original form. But they were written as lectures, not as essays, and they contain digressions and repetitions which it was not possible to remove without completely recasting them.

CONTENTS

x   *Contents*

I

THE MEANING OF STYLE

It is, I believe, a fairly common experience for those who have been engaged for a good many years in the profession of literary criticism, to slip, almost unconsciously, into a condition of mistrust of all their most familiar and general terms. The critic becomes dissatisfied with the vagueness of his activity, or his art; and he will indulge the fantastic dream that it might be reduced to the firm precision of a science. He may even, during this period of dissatisfaction, forget that half the fascination of his task lies in the fact that the terms he uses are fluid and uncertain, and that his success depends upon the compulsive vigour with which he impresses upon them a meaning which shall be exactly fitted to his own intention and unmistakable by his audience.

Whether it is with the vain hope of giving to the language of criticism, like the symbols of mathematics, a constant and invariable significance, or with the more reasonable aim of gaining a more exact control over the instruments of his craft, the critic is preoccupied by an ideal of definition. If he cannot legislate for the republic of letters, and determine the sense in which terms of criticism must be used, he can try to discover and distinguish the senses in which they are used. He invariably finds that the confusion is great.

A favourite habit with a term of criticism is to have two quite easily separable and distinct meanings, and to have, besides, an existence in a kind of limbo, where it partakes a little of these two distinct meanings, even though they are irreconcilable. A remarkable example of this tendency is the word Decadence, which is one of the commonest terms of abuse in criticism.[1] Decadence is primarily a historical term; it is applied to that period in the history of a society when its old institutions are decaying and new ones have not yet been formed, to a period of transition between one social structure, one social idea, and another. The historian looks down from the hilltop of the old order into the valley of disintegration. The second distinct meaning of Decadence is strictly metaphorical. The literary critic uses Decadence to describe a period of literature in which there is a visible transition between one ideal, one set of standards, and another. Thus there was a literary decadence in Europe in the second half of the eighteenth century. I say the literary critic uses the word in this sense, but the statement is rather rash. He ought to use it in this way, but in fact he generally uses it in what may be called a limbo sense. He will apply it indiscriminately to the literature produced in a social decadence—though that literature may be, as literature, the very opposite of decadent—or he will apply it to literature which depicts a life which has some of the qualities of a social decadence; and generally the word will have the effect of an omnibus of opprobrium. Fiddling Nero, *vers libre*, Quartier Latin, horses for consuls, Arabian nights, contempt for the happy ending—all these, and a hundred other nuances are crowded into the word. It cannot possibly contain them all; and even in the practice of those critics who are careful to keep watch over the suggestion of their language the word will be found used in a fashion which presupposes that a literary decadence always accompanies a social decadence—an assumption which is at the least questionable, and very probably quite wrong.

That is a typical fortune for a term of criticism; and the ultimate outcome of an attempt to analyse it rigorously would be typical also. It is obvious that the endeavour

[1] See note.

to clear up the meanings of this quite secondary word would carry us in a few minutes into a region where all the riddles and problems of literary aesthetics lie in wait, like so many sphinxes, for the unwary traveller. Much more will this be so with the discussion of a word like Style.

Consider any one of the famous definitions of Style; you have immediately the sensation that you have been taken out of your depth. The simplicity of Buffon's sentence, 'le style, c'est l'homme même', is utterly deceptive. Flaubert approved of it, and read into it a meaning which, we may be fairly positive, Buffon never intended. And Flaubert himself spent infinite labour in the vain attempt to prove that he himself was an exception to the rule. The more analytical definition of Henri Beyle (Stendhal) sweeps us away immediately into the ether of metaphysics. 'Le style', he says, 'c'est ajouter à une pensée donnée toutes les circonstances propres à produire tout l'effet que doit produire cette pensée.' Style consists in adding to a given thought all the circumstances calculated to produce the whole effect that the thought ought to produce. Much is concealed beneath that little word 'ought'.

A discussion of the word Style, if it were pursued with only a fraction of the rigour of a scientific investigation, would inevitably cover the whole of literary aesthetics and the theory of criticism. Six books would not suffice for the attempt: much less would six lectures. I propose to attempt no more than to ventilate a few of the actual problems that confront a literary critic; to try to formulate a few of the problems he has to make up his mind about. I know that these problems will be, in a sense, artificially isolated; that all kinds of tacit assumptions will be made, some of which I may be able to justify; of others I shall be unconscious. The discussion is bound to be fragmentary and inconclusive. But who has ever said the last word on a problem of literary criticism? And do we even want the last word said?

We may make a little clearing in the jungle by considering the way in which the word Style is commonly used. I think that I detect at least three fairly distinct meanings; they appear in these three sentences. First, 'I know who wrote the article in last week's *Saturday Review*—Mr. Saintsbury. You couldn't mistake the style.' Second, 'Mr. Wilkinson's ideas are interesting; but he must learn to write; at present he has no style.' Third, 'You may call Marlowe bombastic; you may even call him farcical; but one quality outweighs his bombast, his savagery, and his farce—he has style.'

In the first of these sentences 'I know who wrote the article in the *Saturday Review*—Mr. Saintsbury. You couldn't mistake the style', 'style' means that personal idiosyncrasy of expression by which we recognize a writer. Many elements go to make up this individuality. One of the best ways of distinguishing them and discovering the order of their importance is to play that excellent game of guessing the authorship of passages. It is easy to guess Dr. Johnson or Gibbon or Meredith or Henry James; it is much harder to guess Tourneur or Webster or Beaumont and Fletcher; you will probably find yourself fathering any half-dozen lines of the *Maid's Tragedy* on to Shakespeare. You may give ten lines of Webster to Shakespeare; in twenty, however, you will know your man. There is a handling of the long rhythmical period in Shakespeare, a subtlety of harmony, a swift superabundance of metaphor, that not even the greatest of his contemporaries could touch. When the writer speaks in his own person, as the essayist or the critic, you look first to his turn of thought, then to his turn of phrase; when you are dealing with the 'objective' art of the dramatist or the novelist, you look, perhaps, first to his turn of phrase, then to the peculiarity of his vision. Whatever goes to make a man's writing recognizable is included in his style.

To say that a writer has a style in this sense of idiosyncrasy is by no means necessarily to praise him. The individuality of Meredith's style is undeniable; there is a growing body of opinion that it was not a good one. The great Doctor's peculiarities have received the irreverent name of Johnsonese. Henry James's later manner was so much his own that it reminded Mr. H. G. Wells of 'a hippopotamus trying to pick up a pea'. On the other hand, to say that a writer has not a style in this sense is, I think, to condemn him; though it would demand much more skill and learning than most of us possess to pronounce positively on the authorship of an unfamiliar piece of English prose written at the end of the seventeenth century. The *sermo communis* of those days had a limpidity which makes it hard to be sure of the personal nuance.

In the second sentence: 'Mr. Wilkinson's ideas are interesting; but he must learn to write; at present he has no style', the word is used of the technique of expression. This style is the quality which—it is often said—French journalists do, and English journalists do not, possess by nature; the power of lucid exposition of a sequence of ideas. I think that style in this sense can only be properly applied to the exposition of intellectual ideas. I am suggesting that whereas we may with propriety use the sentence 'He has good ideas, but a bad style' of a philosopher or an essayist, it is not applicable to a novelist or a poet. In the first place, novelists and poets, *qua* novelists and poets, do not really have ideas at all, they have perceptions, intuitions, emotional convictions; and secondly, the only evidence that they have true perceptions is the fact that they are conveyed to us in all their particularity. If this is done it is misleading to speak of the style as being good or bad; the novel or the poem has the excellence proper to it. The novel or the poem that is well conceived and badly written is a chimera. 'Tout déroule de la conception', said Flaubert, unconsciously following Aristotle's words of wisdom about plots. If a story or a poem is really well conceived, it is immune from the danger of being badly written; for to conceive a work of creative literature is to conceive it in its particularity. An argument is a different matter; it is concerned with ideas in the logical sense, and these may be expounded either clearly or obscurely, with economy or waste. Style of this kind may be (to some degree at least) taught, as it is taught in France today, and as it was taught in the old schools of rhetoric.

Of course it is true that there are certain general rules of composition that must be observed: one must not be ambiguous, one must avoid solecisms, one's grammar must be reasonably correct. More offences are actually committed against these elementary rules by reputable writers than is generally supposed; and Shakespeare had a perceptible tendency to override grammar altogether in his latest work. But if it is impossible to hold that offences of this kind are anything but offences, except when committed, as most frequently in Shakespeare, for potent dramatic reasons, it is certain that no amount of correctness in grammar and composition is enough to make a positive style, even in the sense of technique of expression.

In the third sentence: 'Marlowe, in spite of his bombast, his savagery and his farce, had style', the word is used absolutely. We do not know precisely what it means; but we know that it means generally that Marlowe could write such lines as

See where Christ's blood streams in the firmament . . .

or,

Sweet Helen, make me immortal with a kiss.
Her lips suck forth my soul: see where it flies.

They are Marlowe's lines. No one else could have written them; not even Shakespeare. When Shakespeare was writing in the style of Marlowe he was incapable of this magnificence; when he became capable of it he had worked out a style of his own, utterly different from Marlowe's. Those lines are recognizably Marlowe's; but when we say that Marlowe had style, we are referring to a quality which transcends all personal idiosyncrasy, yet needs—or seems to need—personal idiosyncrasy in order to be manifested. Style, in this absolute sense, is a complete fusion of the personal and the universal. A great writer is never more intensely and recognizably himself than in his greatest passages; to use a vaguely metaphysical phrase, absolute style is the complete realization of a universal significance in a personal and particular expression.

Here, then, we have three fairly distinct meanings of the word Style disengaged; Style, as personal idiosyncrasy; Style, as technique of exposition; Style, as the highest achievement of literature. The opportunities for confusion are great. We may say that the critic should make clear by his context the sense in which he is using the word; the fact remains that he seldom does—for this reason. The critic, unless he is that very rare and valuable thing, a technical critic, must be to some extent a creative artist in his criticism. The first part of his work is to convey the effect, the whole intellectual and emotional impression made by the work he is criticizing: without this foundation his criticism will be jejune and unsubstantial. In this respect his task is strictly analogous to that of the creative writer. Instead of trying to communicate the emotions liberated in him by a primrose, or life as one mysterious whole, he is trying to recreate in his reader the peculiar emotion aroused in him by a work of literature. He has other things to do besides this, and to do at the same time; but if he is successful in this primary task, it will follow necessarily that the general terms he may use to elucidate his impressions will have a particular colour and quality, if not a definite sense, given to them. If, for example, a critic has been successful in communicating a sense of the majestical, symphonic effect of Milton's *Areopagitica*, and he goes on to talk of its style, he will hardly need to define the meaning of the word. He has already given it a fuller content than any definition can convey. And so it might seem that all attempts to analyse a word so Protean are lost labour. They would be, if all critics were perfect, and all criticisms the complete and rounded works of art which they are by intention. But the perfect critic does not exist, and never has existed; critics succeed sometimes and fail at others; the best of them fail more often than they succeed: and when they are failing, their invariable gesture is to use general terms as a prop to their own defective achievement. Instead of giving their general terms a full and particular content, they use them rather to give an appearance of weight and authority to misty and undecided perceptions.

Then the different meanings contained in the word Style work havoc in the mind both of the critic and the reader. The word slips from one sense into another, until the weary Aristaeus has no more strength to grapple with the old man of the sea. The vital relation of style, in any of its senses, to the particularity of the work of which it is predicated, is weakened and finally severed altogether. Then we find style in the first sense of idiosyncrasy used quite indiscriminately as a term of praise, as though it were really a literary merit for an author to be recognizable at all times and all places in his work: on the whole it is far more likely to be an impertinence. In how many novels of recent years is the all-important dialogue carried on between so many obvious hypostatizations of the novelist's self! Or again, the unaccented style ('style' in our second sense) proper to a lucid exposition of intellectual argument, innocent of all distracting metaphor, with the plastic and emotional suggestion of the words reduced to a minimum, will be considered an excellence in a writer whose chief function it is to give the illusion of life. This is one of the most glaring of the false sophistications prevalent in what we may call superior criticism today. A flat style is supposed to have some aristocratic virtue of its own, no matter to what subject-matter it is applied; to be vivid, on the other hand, is to be vulgar. That is pure heresy, and those writers who, through some deficiency in their own creative vitality or some fear of the contempt of the superior person, embrace it, must inevitably become parochial. They will enjoy a languid sequence of *succès d'estime* in their lives and be quietly forgotten after their deaths.

It is, I think, largely because of the facilities for confusion between various senses of the word Style that the secular misunderstanding, exposed by Sir Walter Raleigh in his famous essay, continues to flourish. The notion that style is applied ornament had its origin, no doubt, in the tradition of the schools of rhetoric in Europe; and in its place in their teaching the conception was not so monstrous as it is today. For the old professors of rhetoric were exclusively engaged in instructing their pupils how to expound an argument or arrange a pleading. Their classification of rhetorical devices was undoubtedly formal and extravagant; still, it is true that the art they were trying to teach with all their cumbersome paraphernalia was one that could to some extent be taught. If they recommended the use of ornament, they also inculcated the importance of a logical structure; and the proof that their theories were not altogether fantastic is the fact that in the country where the tradition has most persisted and most educated men have in their youth been *élèves en rhétorique*, the gift for precise and unobtrusive statement of a logical argument is much more common than it is with us. In England, moreover, where the rhetorical tradition has completely disappeared, it is obvious that we have no excuse for blaming the Middle Ages if we find the conception of style as applied ornament still working confusion in our literature. It is certainly the most popular of all delusions about style. If the notion that to be vivid is to be vulgar is the heresy of the superior person, the heresy of the man in the street, and of not a few men who profess to live several stories above it, is that style is fine writing, a miserable procession of knock-kneed, broken-winded metaphors with a cruel cartload of ponderous, unmeaning polysyllables dragging behind them.

The mere fact that the word Style can be used intelligibly in at least three different senses is quite enough to perpetuate the misconception, in its less outrageous forms, among those who ought to know better. When an attribute attains to the dignity of having several meanings, it begins to take on a life of its own. It sets up a separate establishment, and very soon it hangs out a placard saying that it has no connexion with the firm over the way. Once style has begun to enjoy this independent existence, the delusion, vague and unconscious though it may be, has begun to take root. If style is something separate, what can it be but ornament? The misconception is nourished by the casual phrase of one of the most deliberate of modern writers. Robert Louis Stevenson's confession that he 'played the sedulous ape' is used to give substance to the ghostly entity of a style that wanders about and attaches itself occasionally to a piece of writing. Any one with a sound literary instinct, or an ordinary measure of straightforward sincerity, can lay the ghost for himself in a moment; but it goes off to haunt other people—leader-writers and politicians most of all, but not a few persons of more nominal repute.

Nevertheless, though it is easy at any given moment to eject from our minds the notion that style is ornament, and to bolt the door against it, the notion is persistent. It may come back through the keyhole. Ever since Aristotle's day it has been held—with varying conviction and emphasis—that writing of the highest kind is distinguished by a commanding use of metaphor. Metaphor, if regarded by a prosaic eye, or analysed by a mind which has lost a certain keenness of intuition, does tend to look like ornament. It appears to be something added or applied, a jewel sewn upon the stout fabric of a narrative, so that if it were taken away the fabric would be left as durable and serviceable as it was before. It is true that metaphor has been often, and is most commonly, used in this way; it is also true that certain of our older writers who took a childish delight in incrusting their language with ornamental metaphor have a quaint fascination for a modern reader. Their style is not the less vicious because we find it curious, any more than the growing vogue of mid-Victorian drawing-room furniture acquits the designers of it of detestable taste.

We shall have occasion to discuss the nature of metaphor more exactly; and perhaps it will suffice for the moment to declare my conviction that true metaphor, so far from being an ornament, has very little to do even with an act of comparison. Logically, of course, it is based upon an act of comparison. We all remember the neat little proportion sums in the *Poetics* of Aristotle. But creative literature of the highest kind is not amenable to logical analysis, and in the development of a great master of metaphor like Shakespeare we can watch the gradual overriding of the act of comparison. Metaphor becomes almost a mode of apprehension. Only by regarding metaphor in this light can we really account for the indescribable impression made by Shakespeare's later manner, in which metaphors tumble over one another, yet the effect is not one of confusion, but of swift and constant illumination. Cleopatra says of Antony :

For his bounty,
There was no winter in 't, an autumn 'twas
That grew the more by reaping; his delights
Were dolphin-like, they show'd his back above
The element they liv'd in; in his livery
Walked crowns and crownets, realms and islands were
As plates dropp'd from his pocket.

or again,

It is great
To do that thing that ends all other deeds,
Which shackles accidents, and bolts up change,
Which sleeps, and never palates more the dug,
The beggar's nurse and Caesar's.

To discuss such passages as these would take us too far at present; moreover, the only purpose of these examples is to show how impossible it really is to conceive metaphor as a kind of ornament. Metaphor is the unique expression of a writer's individual vision. The faculty of using it is in itself as simple and direct as the faculty of saying 'Blue' is to the ordinary man when he sees a midsummer sky.

Metaphor, in fact, gives no support to the superstition that style is a kind of ornament; but the superstitition is as stubborn as nature itself. You may pitch it out with a fork, but it returns again and again. And this is why in all the famous definitions of style by writers who knew what they were talking about, the emphasis infallibly falls on what we may call the organic nature of style. The most famous of Buffon's definitions sweeps away the whole mechanism of expression. Style is the man himself. Flaubert, who spent days and weeks in trying to perfect the rhythm of a paragraph, simply left the rhythmical element altogether out of his many definitions of style. It is the writer's individual way of seeing things: 'c'est une manière de voir'. Occasionally, following

Buffon, he will replace *voir* by *penser* or *sentir*, and say that style is the writer's own way of thinking or seeing. And in the same sense Tchehov, the greatest of all writers of short stories, said to Gorky : 'You are an artist . . . You feel superbly, you are plastic; that is, when you describe a thing, you see and touch it with your hands. That is real writing.'

I am not upholding any of these definitions of style as in themselves acceptable, or in any sense final. Criticism, at any rate, is bound to scrutinize the means by which the man himself, his manner of seeing, or his superb feeling, is expressed in language. But these *obiter dicta* of the masters are significant in this respect. They all point the same way; they all lay stress solely on the immediate nature of style; they all reduce the element of art or artifice to nothingness. Those who have read Flaubert's correspondence, which takes one closer than any other book I know to the actual creation of a work of literature, are aware how strange is this constant insistence on feeling in one who toiled so deliberately and excessively after word-perfection as he. The lesson of the masters is really unanimous. Feel, see, they say with one voice, and the rest shall be added unto you.

Perhaps we may use this vague notion to turn the flank of the general confusion on the subject of style, which was manifested in the three different meanings of the words which are current. By accepting the view that the source of style is to be found in a strong and decisive original emotion we can get a closer grasp of the intention that lies under the use of the word as meaning a writer's personal idiosyncrasy. An individual way of feeling and seeing will compel an individual way of using language. A true style must, therefore, be unique, if we understand by the phrase 'a true style' a completely adequate expression in language of a writer's mode of feeling. From this angle idiosyncrasy appears to be essential to style, and therefore at first sight wholly good. But, as a matter of fact, the goodness of an idiosyncrasy of style will depend upon whether it is the expression of genuine individual feeling or not. It is for the reader, who is the critic in embryo, to decide upon this.

We may put the whole question briefly in this way. A style must be individual, because it is the expression of an individual mode of feeling. Some styles will appear more peculiar than others, either because the writer's mode of feeling is unusually remote from the normal mode, or because the particular emotional experiences he is seeking to convey are outside the ordinary range of human experience, or, finally, because the writer, inspired by some impure motive such as vanity or the desire to astonish the bourgeois, has deliberately made his language *outré* and bizarre. This last is the false idiosyncrasy that is affected not only by youth in the effort to appear original, but by grown-up writers also, when the strength of original feeling fails them and their style, deprived of the healthy sap of true emotion, develops a parasitic growth of its own. The test of a true idiosyncrasy of style is that we should feel it to be necessary and inevitable; in it we should be able to catch an immediate reference back to a whole mode of feeling that is consistent with itself. If this reference is perceptible to us, it will be accompanied by a conviction that the peculiarity of style was inevitable, and that the original emotion of which we are made sensible demanded this method of expression and this alone.

This testing of an individual style calls for sensitiveness and, above all, for patience. While it is true that young writers almost invariably, and mature writers not seldom, affect a false idiosyncrasy, which has no true originating emotion behind it, it is equally true that the tendency of criticism is to dismiss all marked originality of style as false. To dismiss a style simply because it is unfamiliar is unpardonable; yet critics have always been inclined to this offence. Even Sainte-Beuve was cavalier to three of his greatest contemporaries: Stendhal, Balzac, and Baudelaire. Critics find it hard to believe they have anything to learn; they refuse to submit themselves with sufficient humility to a new work of literature; they will not have the patience to listen for the undertone of that deeper style which lies beneath the words themselves, 'the soul', as Flaubert said, 'which gives the words their being'. Where this undertone is lacking, oddities and archaisms of language are gratuitous and detestable, but if you have not had the patience to listen whether it is there or not, you dismiss a writer at your peril.

Perhaps it is this lack of patience which accounts for the long delay in recognizing the most splendid piece of English prose written within the last half-century. It is only this year that a second edition of Doughty's *Travels In Arabia Deserta* has been published—thirty-two years since the book originally appeared. Had it not been for the persistence of a single critic—Mr. Edward Garnett—and the more esoteric admiration of some Oxford students of Eastern antiquities, the book would, even today, be practically unknown. I mention it here, for my own honour's sake, and because it is a singularly apt example of a perfect idiosyncrasy of style; at first *Arabia Deserta* is surprising, and to some readers even repellent: submit yourself to it, and you will find that the harshness and the archaism of its language is the inevitable expression of a mode of feeling, absolutely consistent with itself, yet singularly remote from what men of the twentieth century regard as a normal mode. Behind that wonderful account of a strange land, you discover an almost fanatical austerity of feeling—a perfect harmony between the writer's temper, the chosen land of his journeying, and his language. It is a masterpiece of prose. Yet a casual criticism would pronounce it artificial.

Thus it is from the inside that we must approach the question of 'artificiality' of style. If the vital centre of feeling is there, perceptible to us, then we may be sure that what seems artificiality is in reality a triumph of art. When we feel, in the presence of an unfamiliar style, after submitting ourselves to it with patience, that thus and thus alone could a whole mode of experience be conveyed to us, then we have discovered a true work of literature. The artificiality of Charles Lamb is of the same order as the artificiality of Mr. Doughty's prose; though Mr. Doughty's is at once the stronger and the narrower mind: and Charles Lamb and Mr. Doughty are artificial in precisely the same sense that, in what is perhaps a higher order of creative literature, Milton is artificial. It will be clear from these examples that artificiality is a term to be used with the utmost circumspection in the analysis of literary style. Even if we know precisely what we mean when we use the word 'artificial', the suggestion we convey to others is generally derogatory; on the other hand, the word is certainly used by people who are unaware of the vast gulf which separates that artificiality of style which is the natural language of an original and unfamiliar mode of feeling, from that other artificiality which supervenes when the desire for accomplishment is present without any distinctive mode of feeling, or when the capacity of feeling has withered, leaving what was once a natural and healthy method of expression to run riot in a factitious existence of its own. I think, for instance, that you will find not a little of this unhealthy artificiality in the later work both of Meredith and Henry James.

All style is artificial in this sense: that all good styles are achieved by artifice. When we distinguish between good styles equally achieved by artifice by calling some of them artificial and others natural, we are making not so much a literary as a scientific or even an ethical judgement; we are classifying modes of feeling with reference to a normal mode of feeling—common sense, as it was called in the eighteenth century. Within its limits it is a useful method of classification; but its limits are narrow. Very few great writers have approximated to the normal mode of feeling: Chaucer and Tolstoy are the only two that immediately occur to me. After them I can think only of writers of the second rank, like Bunyan and Massinger, and, in our own day, Samuel Butler. Again, a writer like De Quincey, who, in the main, belongs to the same category, will pass clean outside it when he is attempting to convey the abnormal emotional experiences of an opium-eater. For his purpose he was bound to create an artificial style; but it was, in relation to the originating experience, essentially a natural style.

In adopting the notion that style stands in a direct relation to a core or nucleus of emotional and intellectual experience, we have cut away some of the difficulties that seemed to surround one of the most common meanings of the word Style. Style naturally comes to be applied to a writer's idiosyncrasy, because style is the direct expression of an individual mode of experience; and it is not difficut to see that even when this healthy relation between feeling and language has been interrupted, and the vital connecting fibres have decayed, a writer may (and probably will) continue to manifest his idiosyncrasy. Habits of language, once formed to give free play to perceptions and thoughts sufficiently unusual, or sufficiently precise, to compel new and vigorous combinations of words to express them, may become mere conventions, not the less empty and insignificant because they are the peculiar invention of a single man. Some of the most absurd and most rigorous conventions are those imposed, not by society, but by the individual upon himself. The writer in this condition will not lack enthusiastic admirers. It is true, as Coleridge said of Wordsworth, that every original genius has to create the taste by which he is approved. But Wordsworth was himself to show that the taste may be created and the original genius flag. When Wordsworth was hardly more than a pale ghost manipulating the language he had once vivified by strong and unfamiliar perceptions, Wordsworthians were there to discover the hall-mark of genius on his most insignificant orotundities. The hall-mark was there indeed; but it was not the hall-mark of genius.

For if original genius must create its own taste, it generally creates its own sycophants. The coterie is formed of those who mistake the accidents for the essentials of true individuality in style; the esoteric cult is portentously inaugurated; and unless the master is one of those rare spirits, not too common even among masters, who incessantly judge their actual achievement in the ruthless light of their own remote ideal, he may easily be convinced that there is a law of nature to ensure that his latest work must inevitably be his finest, as his devotees are bound to assure him. Not that I suggest this was the case with Wordsworth himself. The cause of his disintegration was not so much the adulation of Wordsworthians as the influence of his own theories upon himself. In the most magnificent piece of critical writing in the English language, Coleridge demonstrated, with a tenderness for his friend's susceptibilities as delicate as his insight into his genius, that Wordsworth's poetical triumphs were gained in spite of his theories of poetical diction. Men of literary genius, in whom the power of theoretical analysis is not very strong, are often more jealous of their theories than they are of their practice. Perhaps the *Biographia Literaria* irritated Wordsworth—we know that he resented it—into the attempt to prove that Coleridge's objections to the theory of natural language were wrong. At any rate from that time forth Wordsworth indulged in it pretty freely; he achieved *simplesse* rather than simplicity. And it is at least arguable that the chief cause of Wordsworth's degeneration was the confusion inherent in a conception which has been a will-o'-the-wisp to European thought from the days of the Greek sophists to those of Rousseau—the conception 'nature'. The gist of Coleridge's case was that Wordsworth had mistaken the natural (that is, the actual) language of men for the language natural to the poet's emotion, that is, the language necessary in order to express it.

Whether Wordsworth's decline was due to this cause or another, the decline is indubitable, and Wordsworth's later poetry may serve as an example of a barren idiosyncrasy of style, when a habit of language or expression is no longer informed by keen perceptions and compelling emotions. One could find examples nearer to our time, and I have already hinted my own belief that both Meredith and Henry James suffered from a similar atrophy of the central, originating powers. Henry James, whose critical prefaces to his novels may some day occupy a place in English literature analogous to (though certainly less important than) the place held by Flaubert's correspondence in French literature, paid the penalty of an undue preoccupation with technique; or perhaps it would be more correct to say that, with the decline of his power of receiving a direct emotional impulse from the life he desired to represent, he transferred the object of his interest to the process of representation. This is a danger that always threatens the extremely conscious literary artist, and it is the more insidious because it is fascinating. Technique begins to assume a life of its own; it is graced by complications, subtleties, and economies which dance inextricable patterns in the void; the work of the novelist slips free of the control of verisimilitude, and, insensibly, he resigns the peculiar privilege of the creative artist, the arduous joy of compelling words to accept a strange content and a new significance, for the subtle but sterile satisfaction of contemplating them as they resolve in obedience to their own law. For a barren idiosyncrasy of style may have recondite forms; instead of being obviously hollow and lifeless, it may present the appearance of luxuriant growth; it may be nurtured by curious and elusive emotions, which are extremely hard to define. Any one who has tried to write has experienced moments when, in the flagging of his own creative effort, his writing seemed to be endowed with a sudden vitality. Word follows word, sentence follows sentence, in swift succession; but so far from being the work of inspiration, on the morrow it appears flabby and lifeless. Imagine that condition refined, in an artist of infinitely greater powers, with an infinitely richer vocabulary upon which the half-automatic process may draw, and I think you have an inkling of the kind of hallucination from which Swinburne sometimes suffered. Or you may have the condition in which a writer's impulse is derived from his delight in contemplating the formal beauty of the intricate design he is engaged in constructing; and this ghostly, almost suprasensual emotion, will take the place of the primary, originating emotion upon which a real vitality of style depends. This I think was not seldom the fate of Henry James. When either of these conditions is present you have not merely an idiosyncrasy, but an hypertrophy of style. It has a sort of vitality; but it is the vitality of a weed or a mushroom, a vitality that we cannot call precisely spurious, but which we certainly cannot call real.

II

THE PSYCHOLOGY OF STYLE

Before it is possible to enter into a detailed discussion of style, we must try to clarify our central conception of the nature of a writer's activity. In my last lecture, I ended by accepting, with what must have seemed an almost indecent haste, the notion that we must look for the origin of true style in a mode of emotional or intellectual experience which is peculiar to each individual writer. Very summarily, I asserted that a true idiosyncrasy of style was the result of an author's success in compelling language to conform to his mode of experience, and that a false idiosyncrasy was produced when the vital reference of language to this mode of experience was lost, or had not yet been found.

I am aware that this account was extremely schematic, and that it neglected the all-important problem *how* the writer compels language to conform to his mode of experience—in other words, the problem of technique in its widest sense. Nevertheless, before attempting to go forward to that fascinating inquiry, let us spend a little more time in examining this conception of an originating emotion.

If the conception has the merit of simplicity, it also has the disadvantage of vagueness; and you will already have caught me in the act of employing 'emotion' and 'mode of experience' as though they were synonymous. I have dilated and contracted the words to suit the convenience of my argument, without pausing to inquire whether this treatment is legitimate. Since the whole of our subsequent discussion of style will be openly or tacitly based on this conception, I should like to try to show that it is fairly satisfactory; that the thin ice on which I propose to skate will bear.

It is easy to accept some such conception in what seems the simplest case of achieved literary art. Most people would agree that the originating emotion was a prime factor in the genesis of a lyrical poem. There is a profound perturbation of the poet's being, of which the occasion may be an object or event in the real world—a particular woman, the west wind, the smaller celandine—or an object or event in the ideal world—a presentiment of immortality, a vision of death or eternity: to this perturbing emotion the poet gives utterance, that is checked from mere exuberance and lifted above the plane of a sensational reaction, by the discipline of rhythm and metre. If the poem that is the result of this reassertion of conscious control over the disturbed being is a very good poem, each word of it will be absolutely relevant to the originating emotion, not merely in virtue of its logical meaning, but of its suggestion: more than this, the rhythm of the poem will be concordant. As an example of the simple case, let us take one of the finest of modern lyrical poems, Mr. Hardy's 'A Broken Appointment':

You did not come,
And marching Time drew on, and wore me numb.—
Yet less for loss of your dear presence there
Than that I thus found lacking in your make
That high compassion which can overbear
Reluctance for pure loving-kindness' sake
Grieved I, when, as the hope-hour stroked its sum,
You did not come.

You love not me,
And love alone can lend you loyalty;
—I know and knew it. But unto the store
Of human deeds divine in all but name
Was it not worth a little hour or more

> To add yet this : Once you, a woman, came
> To soothe a time-torn man; even though it be
> You love me not?

The language in which the emotion is expressed could hardly be more direct and simple. In the first verse there is one inversion—one simple yet tremendous metaphor —'And marching Time drew on and wore me numb'— and one phrase in which words have been compelled by a force there is no escaping to do the poet's purpose— 'As the hope-hour stroked its sum.' The second verse is limpid. The rhythm is absolutely appropriate to the emotion : we hear the step of marching time, and in the short lines which open and clinch each stanza there are the first and the last strokes of the fatal bell. Even though the actual process of composition may be mysterious, we can see the predominant part played by the originating emotion.

But what of a dramatic poem or a novel? After all, lyric poetry is, almost by definition, the medium for the expression of personal emotion; what of the literature that is impersonal? It is clear that we cannot refer a perfect play—for instance, *Antony and Cleopatra*—to an originating emotion as we can Mr. Hardy's poem. *Antony and Cleopatra* had its origin in no single, simple disturbance of the author's being. In the first place, Shakespeare more or less deliberately chose his theme—rather more than less deliberately[1] in this particular case, I think— but, in the crude language of our analysis, that will only mean that the emotional disturbance was self-provoked. The more mysterious aspect is its indubitable complication. It was to cover complicated disturbances of this kind that I introduced the phrase 'modes of experience', which I will now try to elucidate.

The literary artist begins his career with a more than ordinary sensitiveness. Objects and episodes in life,

[1] See note.

B

whether the life of every day or of the mind, produce upon him a deeper and more precise impression than they do upon the ordinary man. As these impressions accumulate, unless the artist is one of the most simple, lyrical type, who reacts directly and completely to each separate impression, they to some extent obliterate and to a greater extent reinforce each other. From them all emerges, at least in the case of an artist destined to mature achievement, a coherent emotional nucleus. This is often consolidated by a kind of speculative thought, which differs from the speculative thought of the philosopher by its working from particular to particular. The creative literary artist does not generalize; or rather, his generalization is not abstract. However much he may think, his attitude to life is predominantly emotional; his thoughts partake much more of the nature of residual emotions, which are symbolized in the objects which aroused them, than of discursive reasoning. Out of the multitude of his vivid perceptions, with their emotional accompaniments, emerges a sense of the quality of life as a whole. It is this sense of, and emphasis upon, a dominant quality pervading the human universe which gives to the work of the great master of literature that unique universality which Matthew Arnold attempted to isolate in his famous criterion of the highest kind of poetry—'criticism of life'.[1] Though I think it would not be difficult to show that Arnold himself was partly hypnotized by the phrase of his own coining, the conception is in itself most valuable. We have, however, to remember that it is half-metaphorical; that a great creative writer does not 'criticize' life, for criticism is a predominantly intellectual activity. It was because Arnold sometimes forgot that 'criticism of life' was only an analogue to the peculiar achievement of the writer, that he was inclined to choose, as his examples of the highest kind of poetry,

[1] See note.

lines which contained a poet's formulated judgement upon life, such as Dante's 'Nessun maggior dolore', which, though magnificent, is not really typical of the supreme excellence of Dante's poetry; or Shakespeare's 'We are such stuff as dreams are made on: and our little life is rounded with a sleep'.[1]

The great writer does not really come to conclusions about life; he discerns a quality in it. His emotions, reinforcing one another, gradually form in him a habit of emotion; certain kinds of objects and incidents impress him with a peculiar weight and significance. This emotional bias or predisposition is what I have ventured to call the writer's 'mode of experience'; it is by virtue of this mysterious accumulation of past emotions that the writer, in his maturity, is able to accomplish the miracle of giving to the particular the weight and force of the universal. 'In certain states of the soul', Baudelaire wrote, 'the profound significance of life is revealed completely in the spectacle, however commonplace, that is before one's eyes: it becomes the symbol of this significance.'[2] The greater the writer, the more continuous does that apprehensive condition of the soul become. And Wordsworth, in the preface to the second edition of *Lyrical Ballads*, has a passage which has always seemed to me infinitely precious for the light it throws on the psychology of the creative writer. 'All good poetry', he says, 'is the spontaneous overflow of powerful feelings: and though this be true, poems to which any value can be attached were never produced on any variety of subjects but by a man who, being possessed *of more than usual organic sensibility*, has also thought long and deeply. For our continued influxes of feeling are modified and directed by our thoughts, *which are indeed the representatives of all our past feelings*; and, as by contemplating the relation of these general representatives to each other, we

[1] [2] See note.

discover what is really important to men, so, by the repetition and continuance of this act, our feelings will be connected with important subjects, till at length, if we be originally possessed of much sensibility, such habits of mind will be produced that, by *obeying blindly and mechanically the impulses of those habits*, we shall describe objects, and utter sentiments, of such a nature and such connexion with each other, that the understanding of the reader must necessarily be in some degree heightened and his affections strengthened and purified.' Wordsworth seems to lay greater stress on the part played by thought in this development of the poetical consciousness than I have done; but, I think that, if you examine more closely the sense in which he is using the words 'thought' and 'thoughts' (which he definitely describes as representatives of all our past feelings) you will see that it is not a rational process with which he is concerned. The thoughts in the mind of a great poet are chiefly the residue of remembered emotions.

I do not wish to imply that discursive thinking plays no part at all in determining the writer's spiritual background, his mental hinterland, as Mr. H. G. Wells calls it; but I am convinced that the part it plays is on the whole a small one, and never—even in the case of the most philosophic poets like Lucretius and Dante, or the most philosophic novelists like Dostoevsky and Thomas Hardy—a dominant part. The meditation of a writer is, in spite of all analogies, different in kind from the meditation of the philosopher or the scientist; it is exercised on a different material and produces different results. A tragic poet is not a pessimistic philosopher, however sternly some critics may insist on treating him as one.

The part played by the intellect in the work of literary creation is essentially subordinate, though its subordinate function may be much more important in one writer than another. Its most characteristic employment is to explicate the large and complex emotional conviction, which is sometimes called 'a writer's philosophy', and may with less danger of misinterpretation be called his 'attitude', the element which determines his mode of experience and gives unity to his work as a whole. Lucretius used the philosophy of Epicurus, Dante the mediaeval conception of the Aristotelian cosmogony; but both those great poets used those intellectual systems as a scaffolding upon which to build an emotional structure. A great satirist like Swift uses the intellect, not to reach rational conclusions, but to expound and convey in detail a complex of very violent emotional reactions; and I would even say that Plato used a tremendous logical apparatus in order to impart to posterity an attitude towards the universe that was not logical at all.

Let us now return to the play or the novel. The poet, in whom (according to our theory) the vivid emotions of youth had been refined into a complex but self-consistent attitude to life, and his emotional bias confirmed into a mode of experience, chooses a plot. Aristotle rightly says everything depends on the choice of a plot—but there are different ways of choosing it. If he is an author who has to get his living by his work, he will have to take into account the taste of the age. If it is an active and enthusiastic age, he will to some extent be in sympathy with its taste. He will be able to choose a plot which may not be at all that he would desire in point of delicacy and subtlety, but lends itself to the bent of his own mode of experience, his emotional predisposition; on the whole we may say that this was the good fortune of Shakespeare, though the Sonnets are evidence that at one time in his career he reproached himself bitterly with having prostituted his genius on work that went against the grain. But where the writer is a perfectly free agent, as Shakespeare occasionally was, his choice of plot will be of a subtler and still more important kind.

The plot he chooses will then be one in which—to use Baudelaire's words—'the deep significance of life reveals itself in its entirety'. Life, in this phrase, means the universe of the writer's experience; its 'deep significance' is the emotional quality which is the common element in the objects and incidents which have habitually made the most precise and profound impression on his mind; a quality that is in part the creation of the poet himself, but in part also a real attribute of the existing world, which needs the sensitiveness of the creative writer in order to be discerned. The plot of the writer of mature genius, who is a completely free agent, will be absolutely in harmony with this quality. For a plot is, after all, in itself only an episode or incident of life, whether it be taken from history or legend, or from the common life of every day, or be the writer's original invention. A plot that is a pure invention is only an incident in an imaginary continuation of the life of history and every day; how little it is the product of an arbitrary fantasy appears from the research of that ingenious Frenchman who tabulated the plots of every work of literature of a certain level of merit, and discovered that there are only thirty-six (or was it thirty-three?) different plots. This incident, then, of historical, actual, or imaginary life, will be as it were saturated with the quality of life which the writer discerns; its various parts and characters will be of such a nature that the writer's accumulation of emotional experience will be able to form itself about them, like crystals about a string dipped into a saturated solution.

And here, in passing, we can see how small is the essential difference between realistic and romantic[1] or imaginative writing. The great realistic writer is of the same nature and pursues the same activity as the great romantic writer. The difference is that the realist chooses his plot from the life of every day, and the romantic from

[1] See note.

an imagined continuation of life into the past (which is history) or into a purely ideal world. The whole question is whether they are great writers or not; if they are, and they have accumulated a harmonized experience to guide them in the choice of a congruous plot, then it is merely the accident of occasion that makes one a realist and the other a romantic; and, for this reason, many of the greatest writers—I had very nearly said all the greatest writers—are both. Shakespeare was both; so was Chaucer; so was Tolstoy, who turned from *Anna Karenina* and *War and Peace* to simple fables and legends; so was Flaubert, who went from *Madame Bovary* to *Salammbô* and from *La Tentation de Saint Antoine* to *L'Éducation sentimentale* without the least consciousness of any real change in his activity; Goethe was both, Swift was both, Hardy was both, Keats intended—as we know from his letters—to be both, Balzac was both, Victor Hugo was both. The great realistic writer must be also a romantic; the great romantic writer also a realist. For after all, what can be more romantic, more evidently miraculous and beyond all rational explanation, than the power to gather up the sense and significance of human life into the story of a woman's love for a man, whether it be Chaucer's Troilus and Cressida, Shakespeare's Antony and Cleopatra, Tolstoy's Vronsky and Anna or Hardy's Tess and Angel Clare? Is it not like the mysterious power

> To see a world in a grain of sand,
> And a heaven in a wild flower,
> Hold infinity in the palm of your hand
> And eternity in an hour?

These, Blake declared, were auguries of innocence. Well, in a sense, the great writer *is* innocent; but it is better to declare that these are auguries of the fullest knowledge that it is given to a man to attain.

Once more I have digressed, in the endeavour to

explain my conviction that great works of objective literature must, no less surely than the personal expression of
the lyric poet or the confidential essayist, be referred back
to a peculiar originating emotion. The emotion will be
infinitely complex in the case of the greatest writers, infinitely difficult to define or to describe, if only for the
simple reason that to express it completely was precisely
the object which the writer set himself to attain. And
even if we say (what is true) that we are trying to capture
it in a different snare, to cast a net of intellectual conceptions round it, the fact remains that the peculiar characteristic of the emotion we are trying to approach is
that it could hardly have been communicated by any
other means than that which the writer chose. We can
achieve an approximation only. As I said before, tragic
poets are not pessimistic philosophers; if they were, they
would have written pessimistic philosophies. The attempt
to transpose emotions of a peculiar kind into intellectual
conceptions of a peculiar kind is inevitable to criticism,
but the dangers of the method are manifest. Unless there
is a perpetual reference back to the uniqueness of the
original which we are trying to elucidate, we shall find
ourselves engaged in the interesting, but slightly irrelevant, occupation of trying to construct a philosophy for
ourselves out of materials which are not our own and do
not really belong to the writer we ascribe them to.

It is the awareness of this danger that lies behind the
safe old rule that a critic is to be judged by his quotations:
not that they are necessarily a proof of his good taste, so
much as a safeguard against abstraction and irrelevancy.
The critic may not be able to define the essential quality
of his author, but he can show that he is aware of it, and
he can remove some of the obstacles that stand in the
way of an immediate contact between this quality and
the reader's mind. In order that he may do this the critic
needs to have an apprehension of the unique and essential

quality of his author; he needs to have frequented him until he is saturated with his mode of experience. He is, in fact, in a position analogous to that of the great writer himself. He, in search of a plot, looks for an incident that shall be completely congruous to his harmonized experience of life; the critic, in search of a quotation, looks for one that shall be completely congruous to his harmonized experience of the author's work. He has become—in all but name—a creative artist in miniature himself. He looks for some conjuncture, some incident in the work of a great writer, which was so precisely fitted to his complex mode of experience that it served in the office of a prism: through it the whole spectrum of his emotions is suddenly concentrated into a ray of intense, pure light—the perfect condensation of a whole universe of experience into a dozen lines, or a hundred words.

These are the greatest heights of style; and it follows, I think, that they can only be recognized indisputably as it were from within. Of course, we respond to many of them at the moment of our first, external contact; to many, but not to all; for although there is a true catholicity in all great literature which can hardly be mistaken even in the most casual contact, the catholicity is of different kinds at different levels of apprehension. This is something of a commonplace, but some commonplaces bear repeating. Literature of genius has to create its own taste, Coleridge said, and that is true of each succeeding generation. Honestly, I think that the only difference between the attitude to Keats today and the attitude towards him when he was buried and his name writ in water a hundred years ago is that he has been slipped into the ranks of the classics. And the real and important meaning of his having been promoted a classic is that readers are prepared to persevere with him: even to the extent of asserting that they have read through the whole of *Endymion* several times with pleasure. This perseverance with a work of literature is misplaced in some cases; in others it is absolutely necessary. Great work simply will not yield up its full significance, its essential beauty, at the first reading; not until you have patiently worked your way into the creative centre can you truly say that you apprehend it; and only when you have truly apprehended a work of literature are you in a position to make positive declarations about its style.

For the highest style is that wherein the two current meanings of the word blend; it is a combination of the maximum of personality with the maximum of impersonality; on the one hand it is a concentration of peculiar and personal emotion, on the other it is a complete projection of this personal emotion into the created thing. I hope that my attempted anatomy of the process by which objective literature is created will have given this apparent paradox some meaning. The manifest dangers of talking about style are two: the danger of talking about the accidents and not the essentials; and, in the endeavour to avoid this, the danger of vague generalization. Style is many things; but the more definable these are, the more capable of being pointed at with the finger, the more remote are they from the central meaning hidden in the word: the expression that is inevitable and organic to an individual mode of experience, an expression which, even when this exact relation has been achieved, rises or falls in the scale of absolute perfection according as the mode of experience expressed is more or less significant and universal—more or less completely embraces, is more or less adequate to, the whole of our human universe. In comparison with this meaning of the word Style, others seem to fade away almost into triviality; for this is the style that is the very pinnacle of the pyramid of art, the end that is the greatest of all as Aristotle would say, at once the supreme achievement and the vital principle of all that is enduring in literature, the surpassing virtue that

makes for many of us some few dozen lines in Shakespeare the most splendid conquest of the human mind.

The culmination of *Antony and Cleopatra* is such a
passage: in the scene of the death of Cleopatra style
reaches an absolute perfection:

> Give me my robe, put on my crown; I have
> Immortal longings in me. Now no more
> The juice of Egypt's grape shall moist this lip.
> Yare, yare, good Iras; quick. Methinks I hear
> Antony call; I see him rouse himself
> To praise my noble act. I hear him mock
> The luck of Caesar, which the gods give men
> To excuse their after wrath. Husband, I come.
> Now to that name my courage prove my title!
> I am fire and air; my other elements
> I give to baser life. So; have you done?
> Come then and take the last warmth of my lips.
> Farewell, kind Charmian; Iras, long farewell.
> Have I the aspic in my lips? Dost fall?
> If thou and nature can so gently part,
> The stroke of death is as a lover's pinch
> Which hurts, and is desired. Dost thou lie still?
> If thus thou vanishest, thou tell'st the world
> It is not worth leave-taking.

Charmian. Dissolve, thick cloud, and rain; that I may say,
  The gods themselves do weep.
Cleopatra   This proves me base:
  If she first meet the curlèd Antony,
  He'll make demand of her and spend that kiss
  Which is my heaven to have. Come, thou mortal wretch,
  With thy sharp teeth this knot intrinsicate
  Of life at once untie. Poor venomous fool,
  Be angry, and dispatch. O! couldst thou speak
  That I might hear thee call great Caesar ass
  Unpolicied.
Charmian.   O eastern star!
Cleopatra.   Peace, peace!

Dost thou not see my baby at my breast,
That sucks the nurse asleep?
Charmian.   O break! O break!
Cleopatra. As sweet as balm, as soft as air, as gentle.
O Antony! Nay, I will take thee too.
What should I stay—   *Dies*
Charmian. In this wild world? So, fare thee well.
Now boast thee, Death, in thy possession lies
A lass unparalleled. Downy windows, close;
And golden Phoebus never be beheld
Of eyes again so royal! Your crown awry;
I'll mend it, and then play.

After all, one can say little of such a passage that is not impertinent: one may point to the extreme subtlety of the orchestration, show how Cleopatra begins with three lines in the grand style 'fitting for a princess descended of so many royal kings' and steps, as it were down from the throne, to more and more intimate emotion—'Husband, I come'—then, by way of a simile that is dramatically perfect, bearing an essential part in the process of the emotional change—'the stroke of death is as a lover's pinch which hurts and is desired'—to the divine jealousy of passionate love—'If she first meet the curlèd Antony, He'll make demand of her, and spend that kiss Which is my heaven to have'—there is more true style in that simple adjective, the *curlèd* Antony, than in many pages of the best our moderns can do—thence through a perfect metaphor, perhaps the most wonderful dramatic metaphor ever used, which in a moment of time consummates the passion of love with a heart-rending irony —'Dost thou not see my baby at my breast, That sucks the nurse asleep?'—to the final rest of the absolute intimacy of love, and death, 'As sweet as balm, as soft as air, as gentle. O Antony!'

And while Cleopatra is making this swift and breathless passage from the dignity of a queen to the perfect intimacy of the lover, Charmian's voice reminds us that a great queen is dying; reminds us most magically of Cleopatra's power and beauty—O Eastern Star!—when the queen herself for a moment rallies into the scornful, careless violence that is part of her. One can hardly speak of an art so mysterious and masterly in such cold terms as contrast; it is a crude anatomizing of the effect to say that it is based on the double contrast of Cleopatra the queen changing into Cleopatra the woman, while Charmian lifts her into the queen again. But if we try to isolate the points at which the style of this perfect and complex passage is concentrated into a single phrase, we must choose first the simile and then the metaphor. Both are crucial; both are extremely simple:

> The stroke of death is as a lover's pinch
> Which hurts and is desired.
> Dost thou not see my baby at my breast,
> That sucks the nurse asleep?

There is nothing of the grand style here; and if it be said that the grand style is inappropriate in such a moment of dramatic emotion, surely, if ever there was a moment which might be said to demand the grand style, it was the setting of the Eastern star. Moreover, Shakespeare deliberately opened the movement in the grand style. There is no mistaking.

> Give me my robe; put on my crown; I have
> Immortal longings in me. Now no more
> The juice of Egypt's grape shall moist this lip.

The technical basis of the whole passage is the passing from the grand style; the leaving the royal note to be sounded by Charmian alone, while Cleopatra becomes pure woman. But the simplicity into which it passes is of a different kind from the simplicity of Lear's

Thou'lt come no more,
Never, never, never, never, never!
Pray you, undo this button.

Those are the simple words that a great king might actually have said: Cleopatra's are not those of a queen, nor are they, in reality, those of a lover. A dying woman does not use such figures of speech; and at the pinnacle of her complex emotion, a Cleopatra would have no language to express it. This very discrepancy between emotion and the actual language of emotion is deliberately and triumphantly used by Shakespeare in the final scene of *Lear*; in the death scene of Cleopatra he achieves the miracle: he makes the language completely adequate to the emotion and yet keeps it simple. The emotion is, to the last drop, *expressed*. And this is chiefly done, as I have said, by using a simile and a metaphor; the secret of them both is that they bring death, the outward and visible sign of the scene, under the sovereignty of love, which is the inward and spiritual grace.

That is the mark of the highest genius and the finest style. Coleridge had remarked this, when he wrote in *Biographia Literaria* that 'images, however beautiful, however faithfully copied from nature, and as accurately represented in words, do not of themselves characterize the poet. They become proofs of original genius only so far as they are modified by a predominant passion, or by associated thoughts or images awakened by that passion'. Coleridge was thinking, I know, of the passion—or as we now say the emotion—predominant in the poet himself. In spite of his enthusiastic admiration for Shakespeare, he had a marked tendency to regard the writer who gave immediate expression to his own mode of experience—the personal writer—as the type and norm of the creative artist in literature. In a sense, he is the type: for it is only possible to understand the writer who projects his mode of experience into a world of his own creation, by reference to the simpler psychology of the personal writer. But Coleridge made the mistake of regarding—in his more abstract considerations at all events —the personal writer as superior to the objective writer. It was not unnatural; the late Remy de Gourmont said truly that 'the whole effort of a sincere man is to erect his personal impressions into universal laws'.

Coleridge himself was a personal poet: his dramatic gift was exceedingly weak. Nevertheless, when we remember his passionate admiration for Shakespeare and his deep insight into Shakespeare's genius as a whole, it is astonishing to read in his *Table Talk* that 'Elegy is the form of poetry natural to the reflective mind. It *may* treat of any subject, but it *must* treat of no subject for itself; but always and exclusively with reference to the poet himself. As he will feel regret for the past or desire for the future, so sorrow and love become the principal themes of elegy. Elegy presents everything as lost and gone, or absent and future. The elegy is the exact opposite of the Homeric epic, in which all is purely external and objective, and the poet is a mere voice.' The unmistakable nuance of superiority in the phrase 'a mere voice' is really naïve, and his contention—in the face of Shakespeare— that elegy is the form of poetry *natural to the reflective mind* quite bewildering. The expression natural to the reflective mind is decided by the depth, the variety, and the comprehensiveness of its reflections, and of the emotions which give them sustenance. When these are very great, no elegiac form can possibly contain them: nothing less than a created world can support them. And the notion that the objective writer is 'a mere voice' is fantastic: the plot is his, the incidents are his, the characters are his. By concealing himself the objective writer is a giant. But Coleridge, we know, always had a hankering after 'a great philosophical poem'. On the whole, it is a good thing he did not write it.

I hope that this somewhat rambling discussion will have made it clear that in my opinion there is no real antithesis between personal and impersonal art: the opposition is a false one. On this false opposition, it is true, a whole literary school was founded last century in France, which has had some influence upon our own literature. But French realism and the French Parnasse were protests against the extravagances of the romantic sensibility— that uncontrolled indulgence of factitious and unimportant personal emotion. You fight a disease with a remedy; but you do not make the remedy your daily food, if you are a sensible man. Nature protests. So in the French realists and the French Parnassians, nature at last protested. The best of them, in spite of their heroic efforts to suppress their personality, could not help expressing it. It is impossible to be an impersonal artist in literature, if you are an artist at all. 'Les productions les plus objectives', as Amiel said, 'ne sont que les expressions d'une âme qui s'objective mieux que les autres, c'est-à-dire qui s'oublie davantage devant les choses, mais elles sont toujours l'expression d'une âme; de là qu'on appelle le style.' Real impersonality is only achieved by the writers of diplomatic dispatches and leading articles in newspapers. But the effort to keep one's personality in the background is for the writer of talent, the writer of genius even, a splendid discipline. It not only saves him from some of the dangers of sentimentality; it enables him to express himself more wholly: it steadies and it frees him, it helps him to explore his own resources and his powers. This was the sound instinct that led Keats to attempt *Endymion*, and later to attempt *Hyperion*, and finally, at the end of his days, to declare that all his past work, and all that he proposed for some years to come, were only to be 'a fine preparation for the *gradus ad Parnassum altissimum*—the writing of a few fine plays'. It is the sense we have of Keats's incessant reaching out towards objectivity, as much as his actual command over language, that makes us feel that he was a poet of a different, and really of a higher order, than Coleridge or Wordsworth or Shelley.

And it is very important that we should keep in mind that not only is impersonal writing in every respect as adequate a vehicle for personal emotion as personal writing: but it is more comprehensive. It can carry more. I emphasize this again, because I consider the doctrine of Matthew Arnold, whom after Coleridge I most admire among English critics, positively misleading. The limited interpretation he gave to his criterion, 'criticism of life', led him inevitably to choose as his examples of the highest poetry lines in which a poet gives utterance to general judgements about life. They are the lines we most easily remember—'We are such stuff' sticks in the mind. Nevertheless, if you get into the habit of regarding these as the greatest poetry, and of using them (as Arnold recommended) as touchstones of poetic excellence, you will simply miss nine-tenths of the most masterly achievements of literary style.

In the very highest kinds of objective literature, such as the passage from *Antony and Cleopatra* I have tried to analyse, it is infinitely difficult to describe the personal mode of experience that manifests itself: we are acutely aware that it is there, but we are encompassed by it rather than encompassing it. The harmony of the scene is so subtle, and the subtlety so inevitable, that we have to content ourselves at the last with our immediate sense of the richness and the rarity of the attitude to life which finds utterance in it. But in objective literature which, though in itself perfect, is conceived in greater simplicity and satisfies a less complex mode of experience in the writer, the individuality is more easily grasped. Shakespeare was, after all, the greatest writer the human race has produced; the commonplace is worth bearing in mind, for when we think of the arduous effort that is necessary to seize a great writer even of the second rank from the centre outwards—a Keats, for instance, or even a Baudelaire—we feel less shame in admitting that to grasp the concrete individuality of Shakespeare may be the labour of a critical lifetime, and be no more than a half-certainty at the end. With others we may feel our way more surely, be encouraged many times with the little shock of delighted recognition which is our greeting to an organically perfect style. Our reaction contains an element over and above the thrill at the contact with beauty; there is besides a sense of capture, of achievement in ourselves. 'I have my man.' He is not very often snared in a purple passage—or at least much less seldom than the anthologists would persuade us; it is not so much a matter of top-notes, as of our artist's being in the middle of the note—the perfect concision of a natural gesture.

Take, for instance, these three verses from the third book of Chaucer's *Troilus and Cressida*—though one might choose from a hundred others in that glorious poem. To Troilus's love-melancholy what old Burton calls 'the last refuge and sweet remedy, to be put in practice in the utmost place', has at last been applied. They have 'been let come together and enjoy one another'. Pandarus—that truly enchanting character—calls at the house in the morning.

> Pandare, a-morwe which that comen was
> Un-to his nece, and gan hir fayre grete,
> Seyde, 'al this night so reynèd it, allas!
> That al my drede is that ye, nece swete,
> Han litel layser had to slepe and mete;
> Al night', quod he, 'hath reyn so do me wake,
> That some of us, I trowe, hir hedes ake.'

> And ner he come, and seyde, 'how stont it now
> This mery morwe, nece, how can ye fare?'
> Criseyde answerde, 'never the bet for yow,

Fox that ye ben, god yeve your herte care!
God helpe me so, ye caused all this fare,
Trow I', quod she, 'for alle your wordes whyte;
O! whoso seeth yow knoweth yow ful lyte!'

With that she gan hir face for to wrye
With the shete, and wex for shame al reed;
And Pandarus gan under for to prye,
And seydé, 'nece, if that I shal ben deed,
Have here a swerde, and smyteth of myn heed.'
With that his arm al sodeynly he thriste
Under hir nekke, and at the laste hir kiste.

This is, to me at least, perfection of style. One may say
that it is only a precise description of an incident. But if
the description of an incident is precise, if it really puts
a clear picture before your eyes, with the economy that
is essential if the outline is not to be blurred—then you
have good style. But how easy it is to talk about such
description, how rare to find it, how hard to achieve it!
That is a question to be considered later. The two qualities
in this passage of Chaucer I wish to stress at the moment
are, first, the astonishing sureness of the psychology concentrated into this incident. It is a significant incident;
it reveals, with a crystal clarity, the characters both of
Cressida and Pandarus. There are no fine shades, no incessant cross-hatching of reservations and qualifications,
nothing of the confused embroidery of the modern
novelist: 'Cressida, still drowsy in the bright morning
light, did not know what to make of her emotions: there
was a sense of shame—of that she was almost sure—but
from how deep in her real being did it rise,' &c. Nothing
at all of the muzzy emotionalism that so often passes for
psychological subtlety: but the emotion and the knowledge conveyed are as delicate as a thread of gold. That
is style. And the second point is the sense we derive
from this simple, objective description of the author's

individuality : his mellow, infinitely tolerant humanity. I
will not attempt to describe it; moreover, I can call in a
line of Theocritus to my aid, from the exquisite seventh
idyll :

καί μ' ἀτρέμας εἶπε σεσαρὼς
ὄμματι μειδιόωντι, γέλως δέ οἱ εἴχετο χείλευς.

(He spoke to me, smiling steady, with a twinkling eye, and
laughter played upon his lips.)

Such was Chaucer's attitude; we feel the steady, kindly
smile irradiating all his work. It was an emotional attitude, a mode of experience which was comprehensive.
Without that, perfection of style is impossible, for it alone
can lend to the particular emotion which the writer has
to express weight and coherence enough to compel language to be subordinate to it. An emotion which has not
the endorsement of an attitude has a trick of dissolving
away in the mere act of expression; it will more often
leave you with fine writing than it will leave you with
style.

III

POETRY AND PROSE

In my last lecture I tried to expand a conception which I put forward in my first. I will repeat the original phrase, not because I attach any particular value to the wording, but because it is central to this discussion of style. I said originally that 'the test of a true individuality of style is that we should feel it to be inevitable; in it we should be able to catch the reference back to a whole mode of experience that is consistent with itself. If this reference is perceptible to us, it will be accompanied by a conviction that the peculiarity of style was necessary, and that the originating emotion of which we are sensible demanded this method of expression and this alone'. In my last lecture I did what I could to bring this somewhat abstract conception down to earth.

Today I propose to examine, more or less in the light of this notion, the familiar distinction between prose and poetry, and to see whether we can gain from this examination any further indications for a more complete and detailed anatomy of style.

It is fairly obvious that this conception of style presupposes that there is no essential difference between prose and poetry. Whether the expression of the comprehensive and self-consistent mode of experience is achieved in the form of prose or verse will depend upon circumstances which are in the main accidental. Indeed, I think that the fashion of the age is perhaps the most important factor. As the Elizabethan age was the age of the drama, the nineteenth century has been the age of the novel. At a certain level of general culture, with certain combinations of economic and social conditions (which it would be well worth while to explore), certain artistic and literary forms impose themselves. These forms the writer is almost compelled to accept, either because he relies on his writing for his living, or because he feels instinctively that he *must* embrace the means necessary to reaching the largest possible audience. When the fates are peculiarly kind, the writer will find himself naturally attracted to the predominant form of the age. I myself make no doubt that Shakespeare was fairly 'comfortable' with the drama; some of the Shakespearians, I think, were not. With the greatest master of English literature now living, Mr. Hardy, it went against the grain to accept the novel form : from the first (he has lately told us) he preferred poetry, and the sureness of his instinct has been abundantly shown by the astonishing poetical achievements of his later years, when the necessity of accepting the novel form no longer existed for him. George Gissing even more reluctantly accepted the novel, and won a minor triumph in a form he detested. In his work you can actually see inclination at war with destiny, and his style (which was naturally that of the scholar handling general ideas) suffered obviously as a result. On the other side, the history of English poetry in the nineteenth century might well be written as the history of an unsuccessful attempt to discover a poetic form that should be as natural to the age as the novel. The greatest poets of the period died while they were still experimenting—Keats, Shelley, and Wordsworth. Browning went farthest on the voyage of exploration. Keats, who realized what the problem was and by the richness of his natural genius had the greatest chance of reaching a conclusion, died at 25. In England the nineteenth century was an age which produced many fine poems, but no poetic finality; and, in my own opinion, we are no farther advanced today towards a solution of the difficulty than we were a century ago.

For if the writer cannot accept the form that is vital

in his own time, he is confronted by the Herculean task of making a form vital by imposing it upon the contemporary taste. At the beginning of last century, poets could still persuade themselves—for the continuous tradition of the theatre had not been really broken since the Commonwealth—that the poetic drama might be resuscitated. On the one hand, they had a theatre where plays in verse were often accepted and occasionally applauded; on the other, all the enthusiasm of their rediscovery of the Elizabethans. The omens looked better than good. And a great deal was at stake. Ever since the Commonwealth, poetry had been dead—dead, I mean, in the most important sense; it had ceased to play an essential part in the social life of the nation as a whole. If it could have been restored in the first thirty years of last century, the history of English literature would, I believe, have been strangely different. You would not now see it culminating in huge, unwieldy works of genius like *The Dynasts* and *The Ring and the Book*; works which are characteristic of their century, because they show the true creative impulse working free from the discipline of an accepted form. We can see from *The Dynasts* that (in spite of its tremendous power of vision and language) Mr. Hardy, on the whole, did well to suppress his personal inclinations, and to submit himself to the convention of his time; he did well to write the Wessex novels to explicate his mode of experience, while using the lyric whenever his emotion offered the opportunity of complete concentration : Browning, likewise, would have done well had he buckled to the novel. But at the best there would have been waste.

It is, I know, idle to speculate on what would have happened if Keats had lived. The speculation is often indulged in; but it seems to me that it generally runs on less interesting lines than it might. A possible mature Keats is to be seen in relation to the century which followed him, in two ways. First, negatively : it seems to me that had he lived to set his work in true perspective, we should not have had Tennyson, Rossetti, and Morris founding their poetry on the passing phase in Keats's developement which is represented by 'La Belle Dame sans Merci'. Second and positively, Keats was the one man who might have restored the poetic drama. His genius was sufficiently rich and humane; he had a springing vein of creative comedy—not the inferior stuff of 'Cap and Bells', but the ripe humour of his letters. And he not only had the gift, but he had the intention. His last considered declaration of his purpose was to write 'a few fine plays'. One can see why Coleridge and Shelley would not have succeeded; neither of them was sufficiently interested in humanity for its own sake. Yet the moment was apparently propitious: how propitious can be judged from the fact that even *Remorse* had a tolerable run, and brought Coleridge £400 in royalties. And in *The Cenci* Shelley had more nearly approached Elizabethan drama than anyone had done for two centuries. If Coleridge and Shelley could do so much, Keats could have done much more, and one cannot help thinking that he might even have reinstated the poetic drama as the natural satisfaction of a social need, and by so doing have made the most elastic and comprehensive of 'poetic' forms vital once more.

If England today needed the poetic drama as much as she needs the novel, we could prophesy a glorious future for our literature. For the difficulty with England is this; it is hardly possible for a writer or great creative genius to adapt himself to the form of the novel as wholeheartedly as, for instance, the great Russian writers did during the last century. The creative mind of Russia then poured itself completely into the novel, not because the Russian mind was less 'poetic' than the English mind during the same period, but because it was not hampered by the remnants of an old and venerable, but no longer truly living, tradition. *War and Peace* is in most valuable senses of the word just as poetic as *The Dynasts*, *The Brothers Karamazov* as *Hamlet*; but whereas the creative mind of Russia in the nineteenth century (like the English mind in the sixteenth) was concentrated into a single pre-dominant form, in the nineteenth century the English mind was distracted between the obvious social predomin-ance of the novel and the intellectual prestige of poetry. The possibilities of poetry and the novel are equally great; but at the present time there is this difference between them, that the popular taste for the novel is in the main a healthy taste, while the popular taste for poetry is not. I would gladly defend that rather provocative statement in detail, but this is not the occasion. My excursion has been long enough already. But another, and perhaps more convincing, way of stating the opinion is this: in the present condition of the general taste no really good novel will go under. The bad ones are the most successful, of course, but the good ones will never wholly fail. With poetry, however, the chances are heavy indeed that the good and original work will simply not be recognized at all. And the reason is that the novel-form is such that a good novel must contain certain elements which appeal to the consciousness at many levels of education; whereas poetry has no such testing form, now that the poetic drama has decayed; it no longer has to appeal to that complete cross-section of society which is represented in the gallery, the pit, and the stalls of the theatre, and to which the novel is addressed. The poetry-reading public is artificial in comparison; its interest and taste in poetry is largely artificial. Its approach to poetry is no longer direct. And, where the approach is not direct, the impact falls askew, and the reaction is erratic and unreliable.

The point of this discursive digression, which I have followed where it led, is in the rather fitful light that has been thrown upon the notion that the literary genius works itself out in the form of prose fiction or poetical fiction, indifferently, and that the form will largely depend upon the taste of the age. What is essential to literary genius of the highest kind is not the prose or the poetry, but the fiction—the imagined world peopled by characters sufficiently various to support that crystallization of a mode of experience which is the act of literary creation. And a criticism which deals in fundamentals, and works by the necessary method of comparison, finds itself moving easily among creative fiction and ignoring (until it comes to deal with the details of language) the difference which is so often regarded as absolute between the form of prose and the form of verse. For instance, the valuable reference of Dickens is to Marlowe and Ben Jonson, and of Mr. Hardy the novelist to Shakespeare: not of Dickens to Thackeray or Mr. Hardy to Meredith. Similarly, on a lower level, a rough equation can be established between the personal essayist and the lyric poet. Where the originating experience is predominantly emotional, there—I believe—it is largely a matter of accident or fashion whether prose or poetry is used for the expression, except that where the emotion is peculiarly intense and peculiarly personal the impulse to poetic expression is predominant. I cannot conceive Shakespeare's *Sonnets* in prose; but I can quite easily conceive some of his plays as novels—I can even imagine that *Hamlet* might have been more completely successful as a novel. In another degree Donne, though he had all the gifts for writing 'metaphysical' prose, was too intense and personal in his emotion to forgo the highly concentrated expression of poetry. For, where the emotion is intensely personal, poetry is the form which gives the maximum of control. Donne's sermons are splendid and in parts almost sublime, but they are curiously uncontrolled; their vehemence is seldom precisely marshalled. They will not really bear comparison with Bossuet's, perhaps not even with

Jeremy Taylor's. Poetic expression was necessary to Donne if he was to get the best out of himself: in prose, *laxis effertur habenis*—he threw the reins on the neck of his personal horrors of Death and Eternity.

There may be something shocking in this doctrine of the interchangeability (within limits) of prose and poetry. Moreover, there is the obvious objection that it neglects the concrete individuality of works of literature. They are what they are, and to imagine them otherwise is to strive after a vain thing: *Hamlet* as a novel would simply not be *Hamlet*. I admit it freely. I am merely suggesting that a quite different *Hamlet* might, as a matter of fact, have given a more completely adequate expression to the emotional content of Shakespeare's mind. I am not urging that we should neglect the fascinating *Hamlet* we have, to 'fly to others that we know not of'; I am only trying to indicate a point of view from which we can get a comprehensive view of literature as a whole, and see the problem of style in its natural articulation instead of looking at it piecemeal. If you hold with conviction that all works of literature have, by some natural law, the form that is inevitable to them, then we are divided indeed; but I do not think that such a conviction will stand the test of our own reactions. The feeling that some even of the indisputably great works of literature are awkward and uncomfortable in their form is common enough. *Hamlet* is one, Wordsworth's *Prelude* is another; *The Ring and the Book* and *The Dynasts* I have already mentioned. But there are two small pieces of evidence worth considering.

The first is that poetry was the original form of literature, and prose a later development. This suggests the simple question: why was prose developed, if not to afford expression to a content which suffered by being thrust into metrical form? Quite early in the history of Greek literature it was felt that a metrical form could

not follow with the proper exactness the forms of logical
thought. The metaphysical hexameters of Parmenides are
one of the earliest examples of a false form. And the
whole huge crop of didactic poetry is really of the same
hybrid kind—a sort of immense fungoid growth out of
the small psychological fact that the best way to remember a word of practical wisdom is to have a jingle
to remember it by. But a metaphysical argument is something different from the content of

> A woman, a dog, and a walnut-tree,
> The more you beat 'em, the better they be.

To force the form of the jingling proverb to hold a chain
of discursive reasoning was merely one of the curious
mistakes which literary evolution, like the other Evolution, is continually making. Apparently it took men a
very long while to discover that the best mnemonic of an
intellectual argument is the logical structure of the argument itself; and when the discovery had been made, it
was continually forgotten.

The second point is this. Though the development of
prose as the vehicle for argument—scientific, philosophical, and legal—was comparatively rapid, it was long
centuries before it was adapted to a content primarily
aesthetic. Even in Elizabethan times, though prose was
nearly always lively and often splendid, it could not compare as an instrument of expression with Elizabethan
blank verse. Bacon, for instance, makes a poor showing
compared to Montaigne. Since the pre-eminent genius of
Shakespeare was not applied to developing prose, another
hundred years were needed to sweat the fat off English
prose, and almost another hundred to give to it the grace
and fertility of an organism in perfect condition. I am
anxious not to be mistaken: the prose of the Authorized
Version of the Bible is superb and majestic, but it is poetic
prose, so is Milton's prose, so is Sir Thomas Browne's. It

is prose that has glorious qualities that are not essential to prose, and has not other less striking qualities which *are* the specific qualities of prose; it has not that absolute precision of statement which is the mark of excellent prose; it has not the flexible, non-insistent rhythm that is proper to prose in the pink of condition; it has not the lithe glancing movement, swiftly and secretly advancing, which is characteristic of prose. It was not until the novel had become firmly established in England that prose could freely develop into a perfect instrument for creative art. Thus there was a whole period when in the absence of a proper instrument, the minor artist, who had not the strength to fashion one for himself, was compelled to use one that did not really suit him. Look at Massinger. His blank verse is nearer to the norm of plain, lucid prose than any actual prose written in his time. It must have been delivered quite conversationally, for to impose a blank verse rhythm upon it would be monstrous, except in the places where Massinger was deliberately ranting. Obviously, Massinger would have been much happier, had he been freed from the obligation of cutting his prose up into lines. But there was no prose as simple and straight-forward as Massinger's would have been, appearing as prose in his day. So he went on writing blank verse which is almost as remote from a true blank verse as was the prose of Congreve. Listen to this blank verse passage from a typical page of Massinger:[1]

Sir, with your pardon, I'll offer my advice. I once observed in a tragedy of ours (in which a murder was acted
to the life) a guilty hearer, forced by the terror of a wounded
conscience, make discovery of that which torture could not
wring from him. Nor can it appear like an impossibility, but
that your father, looking upon a covetous man presented on
the stage, as in a mirror may see his own deformity and loathe
it. Now, could you but persuade the emperor to see a comedy

[1] *Roman Actor*, ii, 1.

we have that's styled *The Cure of Avarice*, and to command your father to be a spectator of it, he shall be so anatomized in the scene, and see himself so personated, the baseness of a self-torturing miserable wretch truly described, that I much hope the object will work compunction in him.

The odd thing is that this blank verse is really excellent prose—lucid, well shaped, and sinewy. Massinger's sentence-management (as Coleridge noted) is beautiful: 'Mais que diable allait-il faire dans cette galère?'

I hope that these considerations will have diminished the apparent paradox of the conception that a writer's choice of prose or poetry for his expression is largely determined by accident, and depends on the fashion of the age in which he lives and the relative development of language in the two forms.

But these considerations themselves were preliminary to a further question. If, as I believe, the comprehensive and self-consistent experience which distinguishes the finest literature can be expressed almost indifferently in prose or poetry, is there a content which necessarily demands prose for its vehicle, and is there a content which necessarily demands poetry? I have already indicated the answer I should give to the second question by a passing reference to Shakespeare's *Sonnets* and to Donne. The first question concerns us now. Is there a content which is specifically the content of prose?

I imagine that it is obvious that exact thinking on any subject necessarily demands prose. The limitations of metre and rhythm and rhyme must be intolerable to it; to be forced to employ circumlocution and paraphrase, every word of which may be fertile in false suggestion, is practically for a logician or a scientist to be compelled to say 'the thing that is not'. Prose is the language of exact thinking; it was made for the purpose; and I suppose that a proposition in Euclid is an elementary example of good style, though in an absolutely non-creative kind.

But prose is the language not merely of exact thinking, but of exact description. A description, whether of a country, a wanted criminal, or the contents of a room, if it is to be exact, must be in prose. Give the botanist a posy of the flowers that Perdita longed for—

> Daffodils,
> That comes before the swallow dares, and take
> The winds of March with beauty; violets dim,
> But sweeter than the lids of Juno's eyes
> Or Cytherea's breath; pale prime-roses,
> That die unmarried, ere they can behold
> Bright Phoebus in his strength, a malady
> Most incident to maids; bold oxlips and
> The crown imperial; lilies of all kinds,
> The flower-de-luce being one—

and he will give you a different description—a description that will enable you to recognize a daffodil and a violet when you see them. It may perhaps, if you are sufficiently familiar with his terms and the realities they stand for, enable you to visualize them, but nothing more. He is not in the least concerned with the emotional effects of which the flowers may be the occasion.

Prose of this kind is prose indeed; but it has no place in a discussion of style except as a type of the extreme, and a background against which to differentiate creative prose. But there are contents of other and more interesting kinds which seem positively to demand prose. Take, for instance, the passage from Massinger, which I deliberately read as prose, because it is to all intents and purposes prose. It is indeed a true prose period :

I once observed in a tragedy of ours, in which a murder was acted to the life, a guilty hearer . . . make discovery of that which torture could not wring from him. Nor can it appear like an impossibility, but that your father, looking upon a covetous man presented on the stage, as in a mirror, may see his own deformity and loathe it. Now, could you but persuade the emperor to see a comedy we have that's styled *The Cure of Avarice*, and to command your father to be a spectator of it, he shall be so anatomized in the scene, and see himself so personated, the baseness of a self-torturing miserable wretch truly described, that I much hope the object will work compunction in him.

In order to distinguish the quality of this more precisely, compare the kindred passage in *Hamlet*:

> I have heard
> That guilty creatures sitting at a play
> Have by the very cunning of the scene
> Been struck so to the soul that presently
> They have proclaimed their malefactions;
> For murder, though it have no tongue, will speak
> With most miraculous organ. I'll have these players
> Play something like the murder of my father
> Before mine uncle. I'll observe his looks,
> I'll tent him to the quick: if he but blench
> I know my course.

The passage from Massinger has a perfect logical structure. Hamlet, who is using exactly the same argument, and laying the same plan, leaps the essential steps to the conclusion, and leaps back again. The difference is one of emotional temperature; the Shakespeare is at boiling-point, the Massinger a few degrees below blood-heat; one is the poetry of passion, the other the prose of calculation. The calculation I mean is in the mind of Massinger, not of his character. Iago calculates, more and more coolly by far than Hamlet, yet his speeches have not any of the deliberate common-sense of Massinger in them; the emotion behind the conception of Iago compels him, at his coldest, to speak with the inward speed of passion. On the other hand, the speech of Hamlet might perfectly well be in prose; but it would be a very different prose from Massinger's. It would not be necessarily and inevitably prose.

This prosaic quality of Massinger, which makes us feel so acutely that the form of his time was unsuited to him, is the direct result of the temperature of his mind. Naturally, he is never at boiling-point; sometimes he feels that he ought to look as though he were boiling, and he begins to rant: then he makes most uncomfortable reading. There was something in Massinger which compelled him to take things coolly; they made no very deep impression upon him. He spent most of his life writing tragedies, for the simple reason that his abilities as a writer were real and tragedy was the fashion. But he was far indeed from having that peculiar sense of the quality of life which makes tragedy a natural expression; his conception of tragedy is utterly artificial; his hero, for example, in *The Virgin Martyr*, is inhumanly and impossibly good. He could work out a tragedy, but he could not conceive one. In other words, his attitude to life was perfectly rational and sane. The standards to which he referred it were not those absolutely personal standards which are derived from the writer's own instinctive reactions, but standards partly inherited, partly derived from the social sense of his time. He responded not to the thing or the event in itself, but to its aberration from the normal.

This was the prosaic quality in Massinger, and it is not surprising to any one who has read his tragedies that his real achievement was in comedy. *A New Way to Pay Old Debts* and *A City Madam* are obviously the most natural form of expression for his talent that the age could give. They, too, happen to be written in verse; but they are really the purest prose. The versification is extremely practised, but quite mechanical. His comedy, as a recent critic has pointed out, has really very little connexion with Elizabethan comedy; it is the direct predecessor of the Restoration comedy. He hovers unsteadily

C

between the old conventions which were unfitted to him and the new which were not yet shaped and which he himself had not the strength to shape; but we can see that his talent was for prose comedy.

The attitude of mind which expresses itself in the comedy of manners is one which demands prose. To see the social comedy at all, to distinguish the excrescences from the polite normality of an age, means that the writer must interpose between his sensitiveness and the world a neutralizing screen of rational judgement. He is not engaged in creating a universe but in readjusting one; the ordering principle of his world is a social convention which he accepts, and with which he identifies himself; he measures men and women by the standard of an ideal, but the ideal is not his own, it is that of the society in which he moves, and if it has become second nature in him, that is because he feels himself freest and most comfortable as a member of society. Not that delicate perceptions are not necessary to the writer of social comedy; but the principle by which those perceptions are ordered does not arise out of the perceptions themselves; the endorsement they receive comes not from the self-consistent attitude refined by the author out of his own impressions, but from an inherited accumulation of social experience. The comedian is the most social of all artists. For his central activity, his measurement of the aberration from an ideal that is not only possible for, but inherent in society, prose, the medium of exactness, is the appropriate instrument. Poetry has no reinforcement to give— the emotional appeal which poetry heightens would be merely a disturbing element, for the comedian's appeal is to the rational judgement of men. Of course, social comedy has been written in verse form as Massinger's was and Molière's, but in these the form is largely irrelevant. No one dreams of calling Molière primarily a poet, and Massinger keeps the name chiefly because he has slipped in among the sacrosanct Elizabethans; while Aristophanes and Ben Jonson are writers of farce, not social comedians at all. The ideal of the art as practised in England lies somewhere between Congreve and Jane Austen. Consider this passage from Jane Austen's earliest novel, *Sense and Sensibility*:

> Marianne's performance was highly applauded. Sir John was loud in his admiration at the end of every song, and as loud in his conversation with the others while every song lasted. Lady Middleton frequently called him to order, wondered how any one's attention could be diverted from the music for a moment, and asked Marianne to sing a particular song which Marianne had just finished. Colonel Brandon alone of all the party heard her without being in raptures. He paid her only the compliment of attention; and she felt a respect for him on the occasion, which the others had reasonably forfeited by their shameless want of taste. His pleasure in music, though it amounted not to that ecstatic delight which alone could sympathize with her own, was estimable when contrasted against the horrible insensibility of the others; and she was reasonable enough to allow that a man of five and thirty might well have outlived all acuteness of feeling and every exquisite power of enjoyment. She was perfectly disposed to make every allowance for the Colonel's advanced state of life which humanity required.

That is, as sportsmen would say, a perfect right and left; the two quite different birds of aberration are beautifully dropped—the social humbug of Sir John and Lady Middleton, and the romantic sensibility of Marianne. The author's point of vantage is central, and for her purpose she personifies it in Colonel Brandon. The use of anything but prose for the expression of such cool perceptions would obviously be not merely an unnecessary but a positively hampering convention. One would simply risk blurring the keen edge. These effects of contrast between the appearance and the reality, between affectation and honesty, demand exactness of language; the rich reward of enhanced emotional suggestion which poetry gives in return for the judicial precision it takes away would only be an encumbrance. The style resides in the exactness with which the perceptions and the scheme to which they are referred are conveyed; these are given at the same moment—the reference to a self-consistent mode of experience is immediately perceptible. It fully satisfies our definition of a true individuality of style : the reason why it is *necessarily* prose is that the mode of experience is not predominantly emotional.

For reasons which are somewhat similar it seems to me that prose is the proper vehicle of satire. Here again the historical fact is that many of the most famous satires have been written in verse—Horace and Juvenal among the ancients, and plenty from Donne to Churchill in English. Nevertheless, the metrical form no more makes the satire of Horace or Hudibras poetry than it did the passage of Massinger which I quoted. The content is almost invariably prosaic, whatever the form may be. Still, there is a meaning in the well-known tag of Juvenal, *Facit indignatio versus*, which makes it worth while to consider for a moment the nature of satire. There is not much doubt that Juvenal was right in saying that the emotion of indignation is fundamental in the satirist; and there is no reason why this disturbance of the emotional being should not find expression in poetry. Indeed, if poetry is (as I have previously suggested) the natural expression of the more violent kinds of personal emotion, it is surely the natural vehicle of indignation. I think immediately of some of the most withering epigrams of Catullus—'Lesbia, illa Lesbia, quam Catullus unam'—to which the rhythmical form is as necessary and inevitable as to any of his love-lyrics. *Facit indignatio versus* is true enough. But personal indignation of this kind, though it is the basis of satire, does not suffice for the real satirical attitude. Satire is not a matter of personal resentment, but of impersonal condemnation. Partly by reason of the classical tradition, invective and true satire are often indiscriminately lumped together under the single name; but they ought to be distinguished. True satire implies the condemnation of a society by reference to an ideal; it differs from invective in that it is not an attack aimed by a particular at a particular—'Of these the false Achitophel was first' is not satire; while it differs from social comedy in that the ideal to which the reference is made is not practical and inherent in society. The comedian is not indignant, because the space between his ideal and the actual can without difficulty be bridged; the satirist is indignant because there is an impassable abyss between the reality and his dream.

Satire is, in short, a kind of metaphysical comedy; and, like comedy, it is based on a method of contrast. The satirist is engaged in measuring the monstrous aberration from the ideal. The aberration is now all on one side : the satirist does not hold a middle point of vantage like the comedian. Nevertheless, he has to keep equally cool, for his activity is predominantly intellectual. His ideal standard of reference was framed in accordance with his emotions, indeed, but the measurement of the aberration from it is an affair of unbiased calculation. The emotion of the satirist has to be suppressed and concealed : the *emportement* of the lampooner or the thundering preacher is impossible for him, for again his appeal is to the rational part of man; he is engaged in a demonstration, and his aim is so to arrange the facts that his hearers, in spite of themselves, are driven to refer them to his own ideal. The famous technical device of the satirist is to compel an ordinary member of society to explain the conventions, institutions, and morality of his country to a being of a superior morality to whom they are unknown : Swift, Voltaire, 'Erewhon' Butler, and of our own contemporaries,

Anatole France and Mr. H. G. Wells, have employed it, and we may almost say that it is the necessary technique of the true satirist. And the conclusion of the superior being is always in much the same terms as the verdict of the King of Brobdingnag on Gulliver's exposition of English society:

My little friend Grildrig, you have made a most admirable panegyric on your country; you have clearly proved that ignorance, idleness, and vice may be sometimes the only ingredients for qualifying a legislator; that laws are best explained, interpreted, and applied by those whose interest and abilities lie in perverting, confounding, and eluding them. I observe among you some lines of an institution, which in its original might have been tolerable, but these half-erased, and the rest wholly blurred and blotted by corruptions. It doth not appear from all you have said, how any one virtue is required toward the procurement of any one station among you; much less that men are ennobled on account of their virtue, that priests are advanced for their piety and learning, soldiers for their conduct or valour, judges for their integrity, or counsellors for their wisdom. As for yourself (continued the king) who have spent the greatest part of your life in travelling, I am well disposed to hope you may hitherto have escaped many vices of your country. But by what I have gathered from your own relation, and the answers I have with much pains wringed and extorted from you, I cannot but conclude the bulk of your natives to be the most pernicious race of little odious vermin ever suffered to crawl upon the surface of the earth.

Such an effect is proper to prose, and possible only in prose; it depends upon the absolute economy of statement, for where the appeal is made to reason, it cannot be heightened by being garnished with an appeal to emotion. Its force will be diminished. No barrister wastes his forensic oratory upon the Law Lords.

The specific virtue of prose is that it is judicial; and

that is a virtue that poetry cannot have: if it has, it is not poetry, but prose in metre. Where the appeal is to the judgement, there the vehicle is prose: if the appeal is made with absolute economy, so that the movement is swift and certain to the conclusion, then it will give an aesthetic pleasure over and above its convincing force. Though it may be too much to say that the finest prose is of this kind, or that perfect prose is only possible when it has to convey a content that is specifically the content of prose, it is worth while to protest against the frequent habit of estimating prose according as it approaches the condition of poetry. I have in mind a recent anthology of English prose, which carries this mistaken notion so far that it gives twenty pages to Charles Lamb and two to Swift; moreover, the anthologist has been at infinite pains to ransack Swift for perhaps the only purple passage he ever permitted himself; and he has done the same for two modern and closely allied masters of plain prose, Samuel Butler and Bernard Shaw. Of such an anthology one can only say that its author is insensitive to some of the most peculiar beauties of prose. But the heresy that the more poetic prose is, the finer it is, is widespread; it should be deplored and combated, not only because it is a vice of taste, but because in practice there is nothing more dangerous to the formation of a prose style than the endeavour to make it poetic. The habit of plastering a plain exposition or a simple narration with empty poetical beauties is very easy to acquire and very hard to unlearn; on the other hand, if you can manage plain prose tolerably well—and that is *not* easy to acquire— you may be confident that you have a safeguard against false emotionalism. Only when the emotional content you have is so urgent that your plain style will not express it, will you be tempted to depart from it; and then you will not be tempted but compelled; and then you will be on the way to a style of your own.

That fine prose is necessarily poetic, that it makes its appeal directly to the emotions, by the apparatus of image and rhythm essential to that appeal, is a heresy; on the other hand, the few purists who maintain that what I have called judicial prose, because it has the virtues and achieves the effects that prose alone can possess or achieve, is therefore to be preferred to all other prose, seem to me quite wrong-headed. They are like those politicians who, in order to rectify injustice to the manual labourer, deny that other classes in the community have any rights at all. As though it were somehow illegitimate that prose, because it alone can appeal to the judgement, should presume to appeal to the emotions! Prose is an instrument whose range is infinite, and probably its possibilities have been less explored than those of poetry. If we look back on the last hundred years not merely of English, but of European literature, it seems to me fairly plain that the bulk of the creative work of the century has been in prose; the bias of the period is definitely towards prose; and this is not, I believe, because of any imagined superiority in prose as a medium—there is no reason to suppose the great writers of the nineteenth century so deluded—but simply because of the changed social conditions. With the rise in the general level of education, and the breakdown of the old semi-feudal aristocracy which accompanied it, came the closing of one economic channel by which literature was kept productive, and the opening of another. At one and the same time the old system of patronage and pensions disappeared, and it became possible for a writer to maintain himself (sometimes almost in opulence) by the sale of prose fiction. (In passing, may I suggest that an extremely valuable work might be done by any one who would devote himself to writing 'An Economic History of English Literature'? Not only is the subject fascinating in itself, but it would supply a most necessary counterpoise to those metaphysical critics who tacitly assume that all writers who have not private incomes live on air, and in virtue of this assumption are able to enjoy the truly Hegelian spectacle of forms evolving out of forms in ever-lasting self-generation. This History needs to be written; for economic causes are as operative in determining the course of literature as they are in turning the current of history.) I was saying that the last century of European literature opened with two decisive changes—the dis-appearance of patronage, and the possibility of making an independent livelihood from prose fiction; and, in spite of all the real and obvious dangers of the popular appeal, literature has benefited by the change. It is always good when a vital relation between a writer and his audience is established. From economic necessity first, and then more positively from the sense of exhilaration which a writer receives from a vital relation with his audience, the bias of the century has been towards prose fiction; and in that time it has been abundantly proved that prose fiction is an instrument at least as adequate to the needs of the great creative genius as the other supreme literary form, the poetic drama.

Possibly it may not be true to say that prose fiction can do all that poetry can do; it is sufficient for my pur-poses if we admit that it can do most of the things that poetry can do, and if we remember that prose fiction is still very young. But I want, if I can, to persuade you to conceive it as a medium analogous to the medium of poetry; as an instrument on which the experiences and emotions that lay behind *Antony and Cleopatra* could find a different, but no less complete, expression. The forms of literature change, but not the form of creative literary genius. A Shakespeare and a Chaucer would have been perfectly happy with our modern fashions and our modern tools; but they would have written things that looked, to the superficial eye at least, very different from the work we know them by. If you find this idea not intolerable, or perhaps even persuasive, you will discover a good reason to mistrust both those who declare that obviously 'poetic' prose is the finest prose, and those who maintain that judicial prose must have the pre-eminence: supreme effects are possible in both kinds. But our conception of prose as an analogous instrument will lead us to suspect that even these two kinds are not exhaustive, but that there are achievements in prose fiction, of description, of dialogue, of dramatic crisis, which fall under neither of these heads, and of course escape the attention of the anthologists; yet their style may satisfy all the requisites of perfection, if not in the same way as the passage from *Antony and Cleopatra* which we have already analysed, in almost the same degree as the passage from Chaucer's *Troilus and Cressida*.

IV

THE CENTRAL PROBLEM OF STYLE

So far I have been dealing, in a large and almost whole-
sale way, with the more general anatomy of style. I have
tried to sketch out a conception in which the various
current meanings of the word have each a share. If I may
roughly resume the substance of my argument in terms
rather different from those I have actually employed, I
will say that 'Style is a quality of language which communicates precisely emotions or thoughts, or a system of
emotions or thoughts, peculiar to the author. Where
thought predominates, there the expression will be in
prose; where emotion predominates, the expression will
be indifferently in prose or poetry, except that in the case
of overwhelming immediate personal emotion the tendency is to find expression in poetry. Style is perfect when
the communication of the thought or emotion is exactly
accomplished; its position in the scale of absolute greatness, however, will depend upon the comprehensiveness
of the system of emotions and thoughts to which the
reference is perceptible.'

It is impossible to avoid ambiguities and vagueness in
such a definition : the material does not admit of definition
in the ordinary sense of he word. I hope, however, that
I have avoided using any term that has not had some
content at least given to it in the course of my previous
lectures. There is, nevertheless, one phrase of which, I
know, I cannot fairly say this. The phrase is vital; everything depends upon it. There, if anywhere, is hidden the
secret of the mystery.

I have spoken 'of language which communicates precisely thoughts and emotions'; I have spent a good deal of

time in trying to elucidate some of the various forms that emotions and thoughts may take in the author's mind: and I have left without investigation, as though it were the most ordinary occurrence in the world, this activity of 'precise communication'. Believe me, I did this without any intention of burking the issue, but simply because to postpone the crucial discussion seemed the only way of keeping a sense of proportion about it. For style wholly depends upon this precise communication; where it is not, style does not exist; yet the danger of trying to grapple with it immediately is that we are left with no criterion to distinguish between the excellences of style. It seems to me a fundamental fact that there is a hierarchy in literature, and therefore in literary style; any critical attempt which affects to ignore this fundamental fact (as a great deal of even the best recent literary criticism has done) is incomplete and unsatisfactory.

After all, you may feel that 'the precise communication of emotion and thought' is really a simple matter. For some obscure reason, it sounds simple; and perhaps in the case of pure thought it is not so difficult. I suppose that Euclid, once he had conceived the forty-seventh proposition of the first book, found it easy enough to write it out. The difficulty lay in conceiving the thing at all. But with this kind of communication of thoughts, or communication of this kind of thoughts, literature has very little to do. Sometimes it is necessary to the articulation of a great work of literature, as the logical argument is necessary to the structure of Plato's *Republic*; but regarded in and for itself it falls outside the scope of the literary art. I am aware that there is such a thing as style in a purely logical argument, and even more perceptibly in the solution of the more abstruse problems of mathematics—Lord Rayleigh's style was elegant, I am told, while Henri Poincaré's had the dazzling brilliance of a flash of lightning—but, having little logic and no mathematics, I am incompetent to discuss these things, so that even though I feel that a competent examination of them might help not a little to an understanding of literary style, they must perforce be left aside.

In literature there is no such thing as pure thought; in literature, thought is always the handmaid of emotion. Even in comedy and satire, where the interposition of thought is most constantly manifest, emotion is the driving impulse; but in these kinds the emotion is restricted, because it has a conventional basis. It is not the less real for that, of course, but it is of a peculiar kind, and needs to be mediated in a peculiar way. But the thought of which we are talking when we speak of it as predominant or subordinate in a work of literature has nothing to do with the pure thought of the logician, the scientist, or the mathematician. The essential quality of pure thought (as far as I understand it at all) is that it should lend itself to complete expression by symbols which have a constant and invariable value. Words, as we all know, are not symbols of this kind; they are inconstant and variable; and I believe that it is rapidly coming to be accepted that the metaphysician who uses ordinary words is merely a bad poet, or a good one. Plato and Spinoza were good poets; Hegel a rather poor one.

The thought that plays a part in literature is systematized emotion, emotion become habitual till it attains the dignity of conviction. The 'fundamental brain-work' of a great play or a great novel is not performed by the reason, pure or practical; even the transcendental essayist is merely engaged in trying to get his emotions on to paper. The most austere psychological analyst, even one who, like Stendhal, really imagined he was exercising *la lo-gique*, is only attempting to get some order into his own instinctive reactions. In one way or another the whole of literature consists in this communication of emotion. How is it done? Let us see what we can do with a simple instance.

At the moment I am writing these words, I am distinctly depressed. I have left the composition of these lectures too long, and I am pressed for time; I am very doubtful whether I shall be able to systematize my emotions. The place where I am living is supposed to be in perpetual sunshine. That is the only reason for living there. The wind is howling; the sky is overcast; and there has not been a really fine day for a fortnight. . . .

I could have gone on for a page or two in this way, and I doubt very much whether I should have given any more definite idea of my emotional state at the moment I wrote those words than I have already done. But what does my reader know of it really? He knows some of the circumstances; by exercising his imagination he can evoke in himself an emotional condition that may be similar to mine; but there is no telling. I have not communicated my emotion to him, for to communicate an emotion means, in fact, to impose an emotion. To do this, I have to find some symbol which will evoke in him an emotional reaction as nearly as possible identical with the emotion I am feeling. Do not mistake me when I say symbol; I use the word because I cannot think of a better at the moment; I mean to include in it any device of expression that is not merely descriptive. The method I used in those few lines was to recapitulate the circumstances, my assumption being that like conditions will produce like effects. But on both sides there is unfortunately an unknown quantity: my temperament is an x, my reader's is a y. The product that results from the combination of those given circumstances with x may be, probably will be, very different from the result of their combination with y. There are only two guarantees that the emotional effect will be approximately the same: the one, that there is a general average of temperament on which similar conditions will produce similar effects; the other, the general limitation of the emotion by the words: 'I am depressed'. Both are vague; both are risky. The mesh of my net, in fact, has been made so wide that it is all Lombard Street to a china orange that the particularity of the emotion is lost.

This, I think, is the central problem of style, as it presents itself to the writer. The question is, how shall he compel others to feel the particularity of his emotion? In this example the emotion is quite simple and quite personal; there is nothing profound or comprehensive about it: we are discussing a most elementary case. But the same principle is involved, the same problem is to be solved in the most complicated cases of all, where the writer's emotions have been systematized into a self-consistent whole, and are being projected on to an appropriate plot that has been formed in his mind. Each separate emotion has to be conveyed in its particularity.

The only definition of style I know which formulates the problem as it presents itself to the writer is that of Henri Beyle (Stendhal), which I have already quoted. It may be said, 'Is not that fact itself rather suspicious—only one?' I reply, 'Not at all.' The fact is that writers, when they deliver themselves upon the subject of style, are hardly ever grappling with the process of their own activity. The conception of style, itself, is a little alien to the mind of the creative writer; it is not a term which he uses naturally. He thinks to himself in a curious, analogical language; he asks himself, 'Is this alive?'; he says, 'I think that's *solid*'; or he wonders, 'Does that make its effect?' Even for a writer who is consciously and deliberately preoccupied with the question of style, there is something awkward and unnatural in confronting his problem under that name. It is as though he had to put on his dress-clothes to talk about a job he does habitually in his oldest jacket. So it is that when writers make pro-

nouncements on, and give definitions of, style, they are
usually moved to do so by some particularly nauseating
critical clap-trap that is going the rounds at the time.
Some harmless and well-meaning lady at a dinner party
repeats something she has read (she has forgotten where)
to the effect that Mr. X has a beautiful style. The rather
reticent professional writer at her side tries to swallow
his indignation and fails: it goes to his head: his cheeks
flush a bright pink. 'Style', he says, 'is the man himself.'
It may have been meant as a withering insult to Mr. X;
it may have been intended as a profession of faith: no one
knows exactly, not even the author.

Most of the famous statements on style belong to this
kind; they are protests. Their obvious bearing is negative,
though their implications are positive. Generally they
mean, 'Don't talk to me about style: there ain't no sich
person. There's good writing and there's bad writing.' To
attempt to separate the element of style in good writing
—well, remember *The Tale of a Tub*: 'Last week I saw
a woman flayed, and you will hardly believe how much
it altered her person for the worse.' The fact is that nine
times out of ten, when a serious author makes use of the
word Style, he is trying, as thousands of his tribe have
tried before, to correct the heresies of the critics: style is
not an isolable quality of writing; it is writing itself. And,
of course, the author is right.

The only thing to do is to drop the word altogether—
I am afraid it has a trick of disappearing from the surface
of these lectures—and turn on the writer, and ask him:
'What is good writing?' The odds are heavy that he will
think gloomily for a minute or two, then wave his hands,
and let loose a flood of discourse in which you will perceive—'rari nantes in gurgite vasto'—phrases of the kind
I have described. 'Well, it has to be solid . . . alive . . .
economical . . . you must get your effect across.' Each of
these phrases is, if you can interpret it, extremely valu-

able; each has a whole semi-conscious theory of artistic creation behind it; but their significance is not on the surface. And it is in the nature of things very seldom that you find a writer whose intelligence is sufficiently cool, or whose power of analysis steady enough, for him to formulate his meaning in terms that are at all precise. Generally you have to be content with casual *obiter dicta*, little examples that linger much longer in the memory than you would have expected of them; as when Anton Tchehov wrote to a writer friend of his who had sent him a story for his opinion : 'Cut out all those pages about the moonlight, and give us instead what you feel about it— the reflection of the moon in a piece of broken bottle'; or when Dostoevsky, in a similar case, said to a writer who had described the throwing of pennies to an organ man in the street below, 'I want to hear that penny *hopping and chinking*'.

Stendhal is the only writer I know who formulated the general proposition of which these are particular instances; and Stendhal was a very peculiar writer indeed. He wrote two of the greatest of all French novels; yet his style—in the most familar sense of the word—was nonexistent. It is absolutely bare, and in many ways astonishingly careless; for instance, he even dared to write that a lady sent her lover *une lettre infinie*. He professed—and I do not think it was a mystification—to spend his mornings studying the Code Napoléon as a model of clear expression; that same Code Napoléon which was to send young Flaubert into a delirium of rage—'quelque chose d'aussi sec, d'aussi dur, d'aussi puant et platement bourgeois que les bancs de bois de l'école où on va s'endurcir les fesses à en entendre l'explication'.[1] Yet, with an instrument shaped after this pattern, Stendhal wrote two novels which belong to the same class as *Madame Bovary*. I do not think that any one has ever more resolutely

[1] *Correspondance*, i., p. 42.

reduced the art of writing to essentials than Stendhal. He had an analytical and critical mind; there was some reason to expect that he would give us the best of all the definitions of style. He did so. Naturally, since Stendhal was the author, it reads *like* a definition. He says in *Racine et Shakespeare*: 'Le style est ceci: Ajouter à une pensée donnée toutes les circonstances propres à produire tout l'effet que doit produire cette pensée.' 'Style is this: to add to a given thought all the circumstances fitted to produce the whole effect that the thought ought to produce.'

The first thing to remember in examining this definition is that 'thought' (as I have said before) does not really mean 'thought'; it is a general term to cover intuitions, convictions, perceptions, and their accompanying emotions before they have undergone the process of artistic expression or ejection. A man like Stendhal, brought up in the French sensationalist philosophy of the late eighteenth century, lumps them all together under the name of thoughts. For instance, the feeling of depression in my simple instance of the practical problem of style, cannot by any courtesy be called a thought; but Stendhal means such things as these; Tchehov's vision of the moonlight, Dostoevsky's of the sounding penny—these are 'thoughts'. The second point is in the phrase, 'the whole effect which the thought ought to produce.' A more truly accurate translation, I think, would be: 'the whole effect which the thought is intended to produce.' At all events, the French hovers between the two meanings. It may occur to someone that a perception, an emotion, a thought naturally will produce the effect it ought, or is intended to, produce; it may seem that it cannot help itself. Express your thought, and it is bound to produce its proper effect. It depends upon what is meant by expression. To return to my crude example: when I wrote 'I am depressed', I may fairly claim to have 'expressed' my thought; but we all know it does not produce its effect.

Ah, but it has to be expressed *precisely*. But mark what happened when I began to try to express it precisely; I did exactly what Stendhal tells me to do. I began to add circumstances. I knew instinctively that I could not give my feeling any more precise *definition*: depression is an ultimate or primary conception in psychology. To communicate the particular quality of my depression, I simply had to try to enable my reader to recreate it for himself.

Now, perhaps, if I were to persevere in that road, I might, after a few pages of laborious analysis, succeed in putting before him enough of the attendant circumstances, enough details of my temperament and environment, for him to appreciate my emotional condition fairly exactly. But life is short, and so is his forbearance; my narrative —for we will suppose that I am at the beginning of a narrative—hangs fire. The proportion will be absolutely lost. The effect of the whole thought, of which this particular emotional incident is only a tiny fragment, would be ruined. The method of simple enumeration may possibly do if I am writing sentimental autobiography (which Heaven forbid!), but it certainly will not do for anything else. The exhaustive method may produce a sort of style, but it is style in deliquescence. I may say that Stendhal's own style was highly concentrated: one might almost call it a tabloid style.

No, the circumstances I have to look for must be somehow charged with the maximum of significance; they must be compact. This emotion has its place in my supposed narrative, but it must not exceed its place: I must on no account shoot beyond my mark—all the effect the thought ought to produce—no less and no more. 'Selection', murmurs the critic. Oh, bother 'selection'; show me what to select, and how. Besides, Stendhal, who had at least the advantage of having written a couple of masterpieces, says 'Add'. Ah, but you have to select what you will add. Select from what? From among the nine hundred and ninety-nine attendant circumstances my laborious analysis would have provided me with. I cannot even wait to review them all; I should lose all contact with the emotion which I trust is to inspire my narrative as a whole. Selection is a broken reed; it is a stout staff only in the belief of those critics who imagine that style is produced by a painful re-polishing of the surface. We know that it is something more intimate and vital than that.

I trust to my mother wit, and try to write my opening paragraph again:

'I am depressed; depressed by the prospect of crowding the work of a year into three weeks; by living sunless in a house and town that were built only for sunshine. A cold wind prowls round the windows. The peach-tree in the garden came into flower too soon; the cold and the wind have stripped it. I too have been premature.'

Please do not imagine that I have the hardihood to present you with that as an achievement of style. The making of specimens to order is bound to be unsatisfactory; but I can see no better way of reducing vagueness to a minimum.

In technical language, the second redaction differs from the first by having been made 'more solid'. It has been pulled together. The period has been compressed and given a little more shape. The effort has also been made to give it a little more life. The wind no longer 'howls', it 'prowls'; which, at any rate, gives one a better idea of the particular beastliness of the wind with which I was afflicted. And I have tried to use the fate of my peach-tree as a sort of symbol of my own mental condition; I have, if you like, 'selected' that from the host of attendant circumstances, though I assure you I did nothing of the kind. The peach-tree seemed to fit my case pretty well; it simply rose up before my mind when I determined to make the attempt to convey the particular quality of my feeling. I was so satisfied with the likeness that I practically identified myself with the tree, and so slipped more or less unconsciously into a metaphor to clinch my period.

From this hot-house specimen of the process of writing one may derive some idea of what Stendhal meant by 'adding to a given thought all the circumstances fitted to produce the whole effect the thought is intended to produce'. Incidentally, this adding of circumstances has involved the adding of at least two metaphors. 'The wind howls' was once a metaphor; but it is so no longer, it has passed into current speech. 'The wind prowls' is a metaphor; but it was not deliberately introduced as one. I was simply in search of a more exactly descriptive word. Precisely the same thing happened with 'I have been premature'. The vision of the tree as typical of the desolating and depressing weather suggested the use of 'premature' as a word more exactly descriptive of my condition than 'depressed', and by the chance it happened that I restored to a word whose metaphorical significance had been lost, its metaphorical freshness. 'Premature' had a picture to give it back its meaning.

I shall return to the subject of metaphor; but, as it is in its natural place here, I should like to emphasize what I previously said in protest against the conception that metaphor is in any useful sense of the word an ornament. A metaphor is the result of the search for a precise epithet. It is no more ornamental than a man's Christian name. For most of the things whose quality a writer wishes to convey there are no precise epithets, simply because he is always engaged in discovering their qualities, and, like the chemist, has to invent names for the elements he discovers. Moreover, I suppose, three-quarters of the epithets we have are old metaphors. Try to be precise, and you are bound to be metaphorical; you simply cannot help establishing affinities between all the provinces of the animate and inanimate world: for the volatile essence you are trying to fix is quality, and in that effort you will inevitably find yourself ransacking heaven and earth for a similitude. That is the simple truth which underlies the Aristotelian dictum on the importance of metaphor; so long, moreover, as we remember that metaphor is essential to precision of language, we shall not be tempted to abuse it. Where a metaphor adds nothing to the precision with which a thought is expressed, then it is unnecessary and to be sacrificed without compunction.

Let us return to our definition. It is, I hope, by now apparent, that the circumstances which a writer must add to his thought to make it completely effective are descriptive and precise, but in a peculiar, and not very obvious way; that the descriptive precision at which he aims is not so much expository as creative. He is not really defining, that is, enabling you to think, but compelling you to feel, in a certain way. If he is a very deliberate artist he will employ all kinds of resources in his effort; he will, for instance, endeavour to give his sentences or his verses a rhythm that will co-operate in and intensify the feeling he is trying to produce. There are some rather hackneyed examples of this device—'The murmuring of innumerable bees', 'The moan of doves in immemorial elms'. Honestly, I don't think much of them. They seem to me clumsy, not very subtle, or very effective. But here is one from Shakespeare that is masterly :

> Be not afeard, the isle is full of noises,
> Sounds and sweet airs, that give delight and hurt not :
> Sometimes a thousand twangling instruments
> Will hum about mine ears; and sometime voices,
> That if I then had waked after long sleep,
> Will make me sleep again, and then in dreaming
> The clouds methought would open and show riches
> Ready to drop on me, that when I wak'd
> I cried to dream again.[1]

[1] *Tempest*, iii. ii. 147.

The musical effect of the dominant falling rhythm, caused by the hypermetrical syllable, is perfect: the complete effect of the thought is produced, and with the more astonishing success, because this little speech of Caliban's is suddenly flung into the drunken scene between Stephano and Trinculo. It is a simpler case of the complex harmony of contrast which we found in *Antony and Cleopatra*. A still more striking example from Shakespeare—more striking because the contrast is achieved completely in two lines—occurs at the end of *Hamlet*:

> Absent thee from felicity awhile,
> And in this harsh world draw thy breath in pain
> To tell my story.[1]

As the now forgotten Daniel Webb pointed out in the middle of the eighteenth century, it is impossible to speak the second line distinctly without drawing one's breath in pain. Coming from the lips of the dying Hamlet, and following the perfectly liquid 'Absent thee from felicity awhile', its effect is doubled; it is the subtle device of a poetic and dramatic genius.

And here is a beautiful example from *Madame Bovary*; Flaubert is describing one of Emma's early meetings with Charles at the Rouault's farm:

> Elle le reconduisait alors jusqu'à le première marche du perron. Lorsqu'on n'avait pas encore amené son cheval, elle restait là. On s'était dit adieu, on ne se parlait plus; le grand air l'entourait, levant pêle-mêle les petits cheveux follets de sa nuque, ou secouant sur sa hanche les cordons de son tablier, qui se tortillaient comme des banderoles. Une fois, par un temps de dégel, l'écorce des arbres suintait dans la cour, la neige sur les couvertures de bâtiments se fondait. Elle était sur le seuil; elle alla chercher son ombrelle, elle l'ouvrit. L'ombrelle, de soie gorge-de-pigeon, que traversait le soleil, éclairait de reflets mobiles la peau blanche de sa figure. Elle

---

[1] *Hamlet*, v. ii. 361.

souriait là-dessous à la chaleur tiède; et on entendait les gouttes
d'eau, une à une, tomber sur la moire tendue.

How the slight echo of those drops falling on the
tightened silk is prolonged in the memory by the sound
of the phrase!

But these devices—an inadequate name for them—
though they can be used with superb effect by the masters,
are subsidiary. Style does not depend upon them, though
it is perfected by them; and in the hands of writers beneath the rank of masters they are very dangerous tools
indeed. How many ambitious writers of prose and poetry
do we see drowning their effect under the waves of a
monotonous and deliberate rhythm? In order that rhyth-
mic effects should be successful they must be differen-
tiated with certainty; and to manage contrasts of rhythm
—without contrast there is no differentiation—with so
much subtlety that they will remain subordinate to the
intellectual suggestion of the words, is the most delicate
work imaginable. It is so easy to allow the sound of a
phrase to overpower the sense, even when the sense is
fairly clear; for when a strong, decided rhythmical movement is running in one's head, it is very hard not to submit to its influence, and blunt the edge of one's phrase by
continually replacing the less by the more sonorous word.
The emotional suggestion of a word does not primarily
reside in its sound, but much rather in the imagery and
literary associations it evokes; and in the vast majority
of those words which can be said to have an independent
musical value, the musical suggestion is at odds with the
meaning. When the musical suggestion is allowed to pre-
dominate, decadence of style has begun. I think you will
find a great many examples of this sacrifice of the true
creativeness of language in Swinburne, and not a few in
that much, and within limits rightly, admired modern
master, Mr. Conrad.

'Distinctness', says Keats, 'should be the poet's luxury.' The essential quality of good writing is precision; that must be kept at its maximum, and the writer who sacrifices one per cent. of precision for a gain of one hundred per cent. in music is on the downward path. After all, it is only reasonable that it should be so. Every art has its peculiar qualities; an artist in language must do everything in his power to realize the unique possibilities of that medium before he summons in the aid of another medium. Music is a superb and self-sufficient art; its unique possibilities are utterly beyond the range of spoken language. The writer who allows himself to be distracted by the musical possibilities of language is like the dog who dropped the bone for the watery shadow.

On the other hand, just as the author must abstain from following after the mirage of an impossible musical perfection, he must not allow himself to be corrupted by trying to emulate the art of painting. If anything is more wearisome than a long passage of so-called musical prose or poetry, it is a long passage of laborious pictorial description: and the two heresies are about equally prevalent.

The difficulty of trying to expose the pictorial heresy is this. It is true that a most valuable quality—an essential quality—of creative writing is something which may be called 'concreteness'. The writer, in his effort after precision, as we have seen, is continually looking for similitudes in other spheres of existence for the thing that he is describing; he is constantly giving as it were a physical turn to the spiritual, and the general effort of metaphor is in this direction. Take for instance, two beautiful Shakespearean metaphors describing that most elusive activity of the mind, thinking in silence. First, the sonnet:

> When to the sessions of sweet silent thought
> I summon up remembrance of things past.

Then, the Queen's description of Hamlet:

> Anon, as patient as the female dove
> When that her golden couplet are disclosed,
> His silence will sit drooping.[1]

In each of these a concrete image is evoked to give definition to the silent thought. There is a crystallization,[2] but
it stops as it were half-way. The image is made to rise
not before the vision but the imagination. You do not
see silent thought sitting on the bench; you do not *see*
silence in the shape of the drooping dove. The images are
bathed in the virtue of the immaterial condition they
define. What has happened is not what seemed at first—
that the spiritual has been brought down to the physical
—but the physical has been taken up to the spiritual. The
lofty but vague reality of the spiritual world has been
suddenly enriched by something of the infinite, concrete
variety of the material world.

This 'crystallization' is central to the effort after precision; it made its appearance, naturally and inevitably, in
that somewhat artificial example of my own invention.
The forms in which it appears are manifold: sometimes
in metaphor, sometimes in a genuine image which we
are intended to visualize, as when, at the end of the voyage to Lilliput, Gulliver relates that the king gave him 'his
picture at full length, which I immediately put into one
of my gloves to keep it from being hurt'—thus Swift sends
us away from Lilliput with a perfectly precise notion of
the size of the inhabitants and of Gulliver. Again, you
have it in that recommendation of Tchehov's which I
quoted, that his friend should 'cut out all those pages about
the moonlight and give us what you really feel about it—
the reflection in a piece of broken bottle'; you get it in
Baudelaire's phrase: 'ces affreuses nuits qui compriment
le cœur comme un papier qu'on froisse'; you get it, in one

---

[1] *Hamlet*, v. i. 308.   [2] See note.

form or another, in all good writing that is creative, because it is the chief of those circumstances which have to be added to a thought in order that it may be completely effective.

In whatever form it occurs, whether metaphor, image, or significant detail, it appears first as a kind of solidification. And writers, in their anxiety to emphasize the supreme importance of this element in a living style, have often been inclined to say that a writer must be 'plastic'. The phrase sometimes occurs in Flaubert's letters, and Flaubert has had, perhaps, a greater influence than any other single person on the ideas of writers during the last thirty years; it occurs in the letter which Tchehov wrote to Gorky, when that writer first appeared: 'You are an artist, you feel superbly, you are plastic; that is, when you describe a thing you see it and touch it with your hands: that is real style.' Though we know what these two writers mean when they speak of being plastic, that is, possessing this power of imaginative 'crystallization', the effect of the phrase has been unfortunate; for it needs only a slight distortion to become positively misleading. And a great many people have been misled. There have been those who have thought that the best way to be 'plastic' is for the poet actually to describe works of plastic art: quite a number of the French Parnassians suffered under that hallucination. There have been others who have imagined that they could become plastic by imitating what they (mistakenly) believed to be the process of the plastic artist, the laborious transcription of all the detail seen by the eye: quite a number of Realists have suffered under that hallucination.

So the old misreading of *ut pictura poesis* has been revived, and still lingers on. It has its origin, in the nineteenth century at all events, in the misunderstanding of such phrases as 'solid' and 'plastic' applied by great writers to the products of their own craft. One would have thought it fairly obvious that these epithets could, in the very nature of the case, only be metaphorical; and that nothing in the way of practical precept could be built upon them. But the understanding of them was made difficult by the fact that an essential element in the best kind of writing is, as I have tried to explain, a kind of crystallization, because that is the only method there is of obtaining the maximum of precision. These two really quite separate notions became confused: a metaphor describing the quality of good writing was confused with the actual process of making metaphors, with unsatisfactory results.

The subject is intricate, and, since I wish to disentangle a further thread from this confusion, I will try to put the matter so far in brief: thus. 'Solid' is a metaphorical epithet applied to writing: it conveys several things—complete economy, complete precision, and over and above these it is understood to imply that the piece of writing has been completely ejected from the author's mind. One of the chief means by which this 'solidity' is achieved is this faculty for discovering a concrete image or a symbol to convey the unique quality of the emotion or thought the writer is trying to communicate. You can see that the critic needs his most delicate instrument in order to keep these conceptions separate, without having a third to complete the tangle. The third distinct conception that insinuates itself is that of 'impersonal' art. A piece of writing from which the recognizable personality of the author is deliberately excluded—and this, again, was promulgated as a necessary ideal by Flaubert in counterblast to the Romantics—may reasonably be, and frequently is, called 'objective'. From 'objective' to 'solid' is a short step, and the step is often taken unconsciously, although there is no reason at all why 'personal' writing should not be every bit as 'solid' as ' impersonal' writing; Chateaubriand's *Mémoires d'Outre-tombe* is quite as 'solid' as *Salammbô*. But, from the conception of impersonality, you quickly get the notion (by one of those slight distortions that continually recur in the history of literary theories) that the author should lavish, or rather immolate, himself upon the description of inanimate objects; you get, in the last resort, the quite sublime inconsequence of Verlaine's 'Est-elle en marbre ou non, la Vénus de Milo?'

Once more the digression has been long and, I fear, complicated: but the notion of an analogy between literature and the plastic arts is generally so dangerous, and yet, in one or two particular figurative usages, so valuable, that it seemed worth the pains to try to separate the entangled threads, above all, since one of the most distinguished of modern French critics, Remy de Gourmont, has roundly declared that the essence of all style worthy the name is the power to visualize. Sooner or later, that very rudimentary half-truth may become part of the English critical stock-in-trade; it is as well to be on our guard against it.

For the endeavour to reduce the gift of style to the faculty of visualization is really a characteristic French attempt after a simple hypothesis to explain very complicated facts. It seems to me that the truth is not so much that an author must himself possess a great power of visualization—even where his gift is mainly descriptive —as that he must possess the power of making his readers see things on occasion. I should have thought that those faculties were very different. If anything, I should say that a writer would be embarrassed by an exceedingly exact visual memory. For a visual memory is, in the nature of things, undiscriminating, and what the descriptive writer has to do is to record some salient feature of what he has seen, which will recreate in the mind of his reader something akin to his own vivid emotional impression.

Moreover, from our brief consideration of the nature of metaphor, it seems fairly clear that the precise visual image plays a very small part in it. What happens, I think, is that a perceived quality in one kind of existence is transferred to define a quality in another kind of existence. To hark back to our examples from Shakespeare, there is no precise visual image of the 'sessions', no definite picture even of 'the drooping dove' evoked; there is an evocation of just so much visual background as will enable us to feel the quality that is being transferred.

What I think we may say is that a great creative writer must have a vast store of these perceptions of quality upon which to draw at will. The more he has, the more precise will his writing be; the more exactly will he be able to communicate the quality of his own emotion, and to arouse a kindred emotion in his readers. In other words, it is necessary, in order that a writer should become a writer of the first rank, that his capacity for sensuous experience of every kind should be practically unlimited. But this is not because his greatness as a writer directly depends upon the range of that experience. His emotional experience, refined into a system of emotional conviction, is of a different kind from sensuous experience; the apprehension of the quality of life as a whole, the power to discern the universal in the particular, and to make the particular a symbol of the universal, which is the distinctive mark of the great writer and is apparent in all great style, is derived not from sensuous perceptions but from emotional contemplation. But sensuous perceptions are necessary for the complete expression of this contemplative experience. The great writer has to carry the articulation of the material world into the world of the spirit; he has to define the indefinable. This is the truth expressed in the familar lines of *A Midsummer-Night's Dream*, which deserve to be more closely examined than

they usually are. Shakespeare did not often speak of his
art : when he did, it was to the point :

> The poet's eye, in a fine frenzy rolling,
> Doth glance from heaven to earth, from earth to heaven;
> And, as imagination bodies forth
> The forms of things unknown, the poet's pen
> Turns them to shapes, and gives to airy nothing
> A local habitation and a name.

For this task, which Science and Logic alike pronounce
impossible, the writer needs an accumulation of vivid sensuous experiences, of perceived qualities with their little
fragments of context. This is the magical language of
literature with which the poet, in prose or verse, utters
secrets which the language of Logic and Science and the
converse of everyday were never designed to convey.

> Poetry alone can tell her dreams,
> With the fine spell of words alone can save
> Imagination from the sable chain
> And dumb enchantment.[1]

But these words are not inherited, neither can they be
learnt. Every work of enduring literature is not so much
a triumph of language as a victory over language: a
sudden injection of life-giving perceptions into a vocabulary that is, but for the energy of the creative writer, perpetually on the verge of exhaustion.

---

[1] Keats, *The Fall of Hyperion.*

V

THE PROCESS OF CREATIVE STYLE

In my last lecture, taking a sentence of Stendhal for my text, I tried to get closer to the problem of creative style; in the course of the approach, I examined two qualities of style which are not infrequently put forward as essential, namely, the musical suggestion of the rhythm, and the visual suggestion of the imagery, and I tried to show that these were subordinate. On the positive side, I tried to show that the essential quality of style was precision; that this precision was not intellectual, not a precision of definition but of emotional suggestion; that there were various methods of achieving it, but that they could all be grouped together under the term 'crystallization'; and I concluded with an attempt to show how this process, and in particular that variety of it which appears in metaphor, called for an unusual capacity for sensuous experience, and depended upon an unusually rich accumulation of sensuous perceptions with which the creative writer could articulate a system of perceptions that was not sensuous at all. I propose in this lecture to return to the charge: I am not expounding a doctrine, I am engaged in a voyage of discovery. I should like to investigate this process of crystallization more closely.

For this purpose, I shall try to analyse some examples as exactly as I can. You may remember that when I approached the crucial point in the process of literary creation, I spoke of 'the discovery of the symbol', by which I meant the discovery of some analogy or similitude for the writer's emotion or thought which would exercise a kind of compulsion upon the mind of the reader, so that, given an ordinary sensibility, he must share the emotion or the experience that the writer intended him to share. I should like to take up the inquiry from that point.

A poem of Mr. Hardy's has recurred to my mind; to me it seems to illuminate the very origins of this process. It is called 'Neutral Tones':

> We stood by a pond that winter day
> And the sun was white, as though chidden of God,
> And a few leaves lay on the starving sod
>   —They had fallen from an ash, and were gray.
>
> Your eyes on me were as eyes that rove
> Over tedious riddles solved years ago;
> And some words played between us to and fro—
>   On which lost the more by our love.
>
> The smile on your mouth was the deadest thing
> Alive enough to have strength to die;
> And a grin of bitterness swept thereby
>   Like an ominous bird a-wing . . .
>
> Since then, keen lessons that love deceives,
> And wrings with wrong, have shaped to me
> Your face, and the God-curst sun, and a tree,
>   And a pond edged with grayish leaves.

That is, I think, a fine poem; but its poetic excellence does not directly concern me now; it is the process of mind revealed in the last stanza. There the poet declares that he concentrates a whole world of experience into a simple vision: the feeling of bitterness of love shapes into its symbol: 'Your face, and the God-curst sun, and a tree, and a pond edged with grayish leaves.' A mental process of this kind is familiar to most people. At an emotional crisis in their lives some part of their material surroundings seems to be involved in their emotion; some material circumstance suddenly appears to be strangely appropriate, appropriate even by its very incongruousness, to their

D

stress of soul; their emotion seems to flow out and crystal-
lize about this circumstance, so that for ever after the
circumstance has the power of summoning up and re-
creating the emotion by which it was once touched. It
gives to that emotion a preciseness which is never
possessed by emotions which did not find their symbol.

Suppose now we imagine that capacity for emotional
disturbance expanded and refined, and conceive a sensibility which is violently perturbed by a far greater number
of individual sensuous experiences than that of the ordinary man—a sensibility upon which the objects and
incidents of life are sufficient in themselves to cause an
emotional shock with a quality of its own. The object is
at once the cause and the symbol of the emotion; having
their natural symbols, these emotions become precise, and
remain distinguishable, while those of the average man,
if indeed they were ever distinguishable, leave no trace
in the memory. The man of heightened sensibility—'more
than ordinary sensibility' in Wordsworth's phrase—has,
as it were, a vast vocabulary of symbols on which to
draw. When he desires to communicate his emotions and
thoughts he has at his command the means of giving them
precision; he can call to his aid the symbol of a kindred
emotion. But that, you will say, is a language peculiar to
himself: no one else can understand it. It is not really so.
The objects have become the symbols of the emotions;
but they were also the causes of them; and, more important still, when these symbols are used to make precise
other similar, but different, emotions, their meaning is
circumscribed, it must point in the direction of the
emotion they are used to reinforce. That is what I mean
when I speak of metaphor and simile as a kind of crystallization.

In metaphor we have this process of crystallization in
its most elaborate form; in the work of a very great poet
it is going on incessantly, incessantly altering and trans-

forming language. But this same process has simpler forms, some that are simpler in the sense of being more monumental, some simpler because they are more naïve.

To take the more naïve form first. Imagine a man with this more than ordinary sensibility, but without the other faculty of enlarging and refining his impressions until they comprehend life as a whole—that faculty which I suggested was the distinguishing mark of the writer of the highest rank, and recognizable in all great styles. This man will have neither the impulse nor the ability to fashion a plot or create a world in which a complex and comprehensive sense of the quality of life can find expression; his emotional reactions, however acute, will be episodic. He will react to the stimulus, and that will be the end. His genius will be purely lyrical, though of course he may quite well be writing prose. An object or an incident in life arouses an overwhelming emotion in him, and a desire to express the emotion. The crystallization is, as it were, automatically accomplished; for the only way he can communicate his emotion is by describing the objects which aroused it. If his emotion was a true one, the vividness and particularity of his description will carry it over to us. Take as an example of this pure and limpid lyricism some characteristic lines of a poet whom the piety of two young Oxford men has lately restored to the world—John Clare :

> To note on hedgerow baulks in moisture sprent
>   The jetty snail creep from the mossy thorn
> With earnest heed and tremulous intent.
>   Frail brother of the morn,
> That from the tiny bents and misted leaves
>   Withdraws his timid horn
> And fearful vision weaves.

The language is perfectly simple, it is also perfectly precise. Even without that exquisite little apostrophe 'Frail brother of the morn', the absolute exactness of the language is a guarantee of the emotion. Only a man who loved the snail could possibly have such a delicate knowledge of it. Thus, quite simply, the cause of the emotion becomes the symbol. The miracle is accomplished. There we have, in the simplest lyricism, the achievement of perfect style.

In a greater poet that simple perception, that emotion and its symbol, would be an item in his store of perceptions; stored up, waiting its time to be employed in the crystallization of some more comprehensive and recondite perception, to be used perhaps as the young Shakespeare used it, to compel us to feel the shrinking of Venus' eyes at the sight of the murdered Adonis:

> Or, as the snail, whose tender horns being hit,
> Shrinks backward in his shelly cave with pain,
> And there all smothered up in shade doth sit,
> Long after fearing to creep forth again.
> So at his bloody view her eyes are fled
> Into the deep, dark cabins of her head.[1]

In the verse of Clare we have the true poetic activity, which is at the root of literature and literary style, in its least complicated form.

This primary form of 'crystallization' occurs everywhere. Where there is a true emotional reaction to the objects of the external world, there is also a keen sensuous perception; and the vividness of the perception is the warrant of the genuineness of the emotion. All good descriptive writing is based on this activity, which is quite easily to be distinguished from the deliberate accumulation of detail which so often passes under the name. For in the latter case, the detail, having been the cause of no keen emotion in the writer, can awaken none in the reader; while in the former, the vividness with which the

---

[1] *Venus and Adonis*, 1033.

object was revealed to the writer imparts to it a relief, a prominence of the essential parts, which is completely absent from the matter-of-fact vision of the professional accumulator of details. Here is a piece of true descriptive writing from a book recently published.[1]

I remember a black sofa, which smelt of dust, an antimacassar over its head. That sofa would wake to squeak tales if I stood on it to inspect the model of a ship in yellow ivory, resting on a wall-bracket above. There were many old shells in the polished brass fender, some with thick orange lips and spotted backs; others were spirals of mother-o'-pearl, which took different colours for every way you held them. You could get the only sound in the room by putting the shells to your ear. Like the people of the portraits, it was impossible to believe the shells had ever lived. The inside of the grate was filled with white paper, and the trickles of fine dust which rested in its crevices would start and run stealthily when people walked in the next room.

The detail is, as we say, significant: in other words, the sensuous perceptions were the cause of the writer's emotion. He put a shell to his ear, and felt suddenly 'This is the only sound': he saw the trickles of coaldust running, and he felt 'How this room is still and motionless'. So that those perceptions, and those objects, were in a vital relation to his emotional sense of the quality of the room; it was crystallized about them. We may remember the word of advice given by Tchehov to his friend: 'Cut out all those pages about the moonlight. Give us what you feel—the reflection of the moon in a piece of broken bottle.' There is also the *salto mortale* that separates true descriptive style from false. As an example of the false kind I will take a paragraph from a recent book by an English writer much more famous than Mr. Tomlinson— Mr. Arnold Bennett. It is called 'At the Quai d'Orsay

[1] *London River*, by H. W. Tomlinson, p. 59.

Terminus, Paris', and occurs in *Things That Have Interested Me.*[1]

It was 3 o'clock and already dusk. I ordered tea on the *terrasse* of the Station café within the station. It is a very good café. You could judge by the crystalline cleanness of the decanters. A middle-aged man sat down, drank a red liquid, paid, and departed instantly. Two workmen simultaneously ascended the two sides of a high ladder and began to adjust an arc-lamp up in the air. From the floor below there was such a continual rumbling of trains that it was a little difficult to hear speech on the *terrasse*. All the big lamps lighted themselves, as it were, clumsily and uncertainly; and there was a complicated change in the values beneath the great arches of the roof. But the vast glazed end of the station showed silvery light for a long time afterwards. Faint clouds of steam rose occasionally from below, and through these the electricity would shine like the sun through fog. The activities of the station were very numerous. The Paris Directory was constantly being consulted; also the exceedingly foul *Chaix* railway guide. The slot machines for platform tickets functioned all the time. The latest telegraphic news was pinned up at intervals; the meteorological news had a separate board. The evening papers arrived at the two bookstalls and were separated and folded on special folding tables. Two tobacco shanties, one in charge of a young girl and the other of a woman, did ceaseless business. Similarly with bon-bons at another booth. A wagon-buffet, with chiefly flasks of liqueurs, trundled eternally to and fro. Luggage-lifts full of luggage kept ascending and descending. . . .

And so on; there is a good deal more of it. I do not wish to concern myself with the downright wickedness of some of the writing—words used with a careless ambiguity, such as 'the telegraphic news pinned up *at intervals*'—intervals of time or space? The papers were 'folded on special folding tables'—did the tables fold, or were they tables for folding? Such ambiguities as these

[1] p. 240.

would of course disfigure any writing; but though they are inexcusable they would not kill a piece of writing where the sensuous perceptions had been the cause of an emotion. But the objects Mr. Arnold Bennett saw had no vital relation to his emotional sense of the quality of place he is describing; we conclude immediately that he had no emotional sense of it at all. To use his own phrase: he was merely 'functioning all the time', mechanically ticking off, like a surveyor's clerk, the inventory of a furnished house. Not a single object arouses an impression or emotion in us; and think of the writer's declaration of bankruptcy in the phrase: 'There was a complicated change in the values beneath the great arches of the roof.' To use the jargon of another art to cover his own inability or reluctance to compel us to feel the quality of that change in light and shade! When a writer, who has done highly distinguished work, falls into this condition, he had better hand over his fountain-pen and his note-books to a new generation. He is in the last stages of *scribendi cacoethes*, the most awful disease to which the professional writer can succumb.

In order to make still more apparent, if I can, the vital difference between true and false descriptive writing, I will quote again from a contemporary author. Mr. Arnold Bennett's decrepitude shall be flanked by the vigour of two literary artists in their prime. Here is a passage from a recent short story:[1]

After tea Kezia wandered back to their own house. Slowly she walked up the back steps, and through the scullery into the kitchen. Nothing was left in it but a lump of gritty yellow soap in one corner of the kitchen window sill and a piece of flannel stained by a blue-bag in another. The fireplace was choked up with rubbish. She poked among it but found nothing except a hair-tidy with a heart painted on it that had belonged to the servant girl. Even that she left lying, and she

[1] *Bliss*, by Katherine Mansfield, p. 5.

trailed through the narrow passage into the drawing-room. The Venetian blind was pulled down but not drawn close. Long pencil rays of sunlight shone through and the wavy shadow of a bush outside danced on the gold lines. Now it was still, now it began to flutter again, and now it came almost as far as her feet. Zoom! Zoom! a blue-bottle knocked against the ceiling; the carpet-tacks had little bits of red fluff sticking to them.

Think now of Stendhal's definition of style: 'Le style est ceci: ajouter à une pensée donnée toutes les circonstances propres à produire tout l'effet que doit produire cette pensée.' There it is done, not mechanically—the defect of a definition of creative style is that it suggests that the process is a little mechanical—but naturally, in the way I have tried to analyse. The sensuous perceptions have aroused an emotional apprehension of the still solitude of the abandoned room; the objects being in an active relation to the emotion, the emotion is crystallized about them. There is no need of those descriptive adjectives, those languid and colourless adverbs which are the refuge of the writer who has not 'the vision and the faculty divine'. 'Magic of style is creative:' wrote Arnold, 'its possessor himself creates, and he inspires and enables his reader in some sort to create after him. And creation gives the sense of life and joy: hence its extraordinary value.' The creative writer does not make assertions about the reality he describes, or predicate of it that it possessed such and such qualities; at least, if he does so, he knows that he has to prove his assertion, and to make his reader feel that it was truly so. 'You have not enough restraint', Tchehov once wrote to Gorky. 'You are like a spectator at the theatre who expresses his transports with so little restraint that he prevents himself and other people from listening to the play. This lack of restraint is particularly felt in the description of nature with which you interrupt your dialogues; when one reads those descriptions, one

wishes they were more compact, shorter. The frequent
mention of tenderness, whispering, velvetiness, and so on,
gives those descriptions a rhetorical and monotonous character—and they make one feel cold and almost exhaust
one.' Tchehov's figure is valuable: the function of the
writer is to enable us to listen to the play, a play which
we should never have seen or heard ourselves, which
would have passed us by indistinguishable in the stream
of life, had not the man of more than ordinary sensibility
been there to perceive it and be thrilled by it. What he
has discerned with keen emotion carries a like emotion to
our minds.

So much for the primary form of crystallization, which
appears by itself in the simple lyric and the descriptive
essay, but more often is to be found in the articulation
of more complex works of literature, where, like the
more subtle form of crystallization which is manifested
in metaphor, it is accessary to another crystallization, of
a large and structural kind.

Imagine, now, that our writer is profoundly moved not
by a single object or group of objects in the physical
world, but by some incident of human life of which he
has been the chance spectator. Again his sensuous perceptions are keen and precise; he has a vivid delight in
the physical particularity of the persons engaged; but over
and above this he has an acute sense of the psychological
quality of the incident. This sense he has may be quite
disproportionate to the actual significance of the event,
he may have invested it with meanings that are remote
from the consciousness of the participants; it may appear
to him as a revelation, a manifestation of some quality,
gay and delightful, ironic or tragic, that he has felt as
the result of past experiences to be a constant thread in
the manifold texture of life; once more there is a crystallization. The cause of his emotion becomes the symbol,
just as Wordsworth's chance encounter with the Leech-

Gatherer awakened in him emotions out of all rational proportion to their object:

> The old Man still stood talking by my side;
> But now his voice to me was like a stream
> Scarce heard; nor word from word could I divide;
> And the whole body of the Man did seem
> Like one whom I had met with in a dream . . .
>
> While he was talking thus, the lonely place,
> The old Man's shape, and speech—all troubled me:
> In my mind's eye I seemed to see him pace
> About the weary moors continually,
> Wandering about alone and silently.

Resolution and Independence might have been a great poem; instead it is a great ruin. Wordsworth makes us feel that the leech-gatherer appeared to him with the significance of a Titan; that some profound emotional turmoil had been disturbing the poet's depths; and that this emotion found some symbolic satisfaction in the figure of the old man. But Wordsworth's moral preoccupation was too much for him: the tone of the ending is absolutely discordant with the emotion he has aroused in us by his symbol. From the heights of imaginative perception we are forced to descend to the level of Samuel Smiles.

But the creative process of the poem was complete before Wordsworth chose to ruin it: nothing needs to be added, only discrepant and unworthy things to be taken away, and the poem may stand as a fine example of that activity of crystallization which is the origin of the highest kind of plot. 'Dans certains états de l'âme presque surnaturals', says Baudelaire in his Journal, 'la profondeur de la vie se révèle tout entière dans le spectacle, si ordinaire qu'il soit, qu'on a sous les yeux. Il en devient le symbole.'[1]

---

[1] *Journaux intimes*, p. 23.

We have but to imagine the actual life of the present extending into the world of the imagination, whether re-created from the past or invented, to conceive the part this process plays in forming the structure of all great works of art. Sometimes, even often, the original crystallization is not complete. Instead of being free to let a completely adequate structure form in his mind, to wait for the emergence of the incident, real, historical, or invented, which he will recognize, by the vividness and depth of his own emotion, as peculiarly his own, and as the perfect symbol of all the emotion latent in himself, the writer may be compelled by the predilections of the popular taste to accept an alien structure; or—and this happens more frequently under modern conditions of literary production, while the former compulsion was more common in Elizabethan days—he will be compelled to hasten unduly a process which can never be wholly under the command of his consciousness. An arbitrary invention either supplements or supplants the product of a natural growth. That is why works of perfect literary style are perhaps rarer than they should be in a country which has been before all others prolific in literary genius.

For a work of literature to have the perfect style that exists, for instance, in *King Lear* or *Antony and Cleopatra*, the crystallization has to be complete on every plane, in the first and fundamental creation of the plot, in the realization of the characters themselves, and in the language which they speak, or by which they are described. And this process, though on every plane it is of the same kind, is different on each. A man may have the power to attain to an emotional comprehension of life, and to frame or recognize a plot that is an adequate and natural symbol of it, but he may be poor in the faculty of vivid sensuous perception which alone will enable him to cover the skeleton with the living flesh and blood of a style that is vital in all its parts: Wordsworth as a poet and Balzac as a novelist suffered from this disability. In their work one can more often see the large, bony structure of great literature, than literature that is actually great; the foundations more often than the achievement of a perfect style. On the other hand, there have been many men with the faculty of vivid sensuous perception who have more or less wholly lacked the power of attaining to any comprehension of life. They are chained to the universe of particulars: within that universe they are truly creative, and their style has all the perfection that is possible within their limitations. But who would hesitate to pronounce between the perfect style of these minor artists and the imperfect style of a Wordsworth and a Balzac?

The combination of gifts necessary to the greatest writers seems more miraculous the more nearly we endeavour to approach them. The incessant victory over language that we can watch Shakespeare winning by virtue of a wealth of sensuous perceptions surely unparalleled in human history, his unprecedented power of keeping this overcharged, exploded, tense, swollen language supple under his fingers so that it will follow the contour of the most ethereal emotion—it is as much as we can do to observe the process at all. 'Others abide our question—thou art free': it is only a little more than the truth. We have the habit of saying together: Shakespeare and Milton, or Shakespeare and Dante, or Shakespeare and Homer. I think it must be because we are uncomfortable at the thought of leaving him unparagoned: a Homer, a Dante, or a Milton is a kind of stepping-stone, or rather a connecting chain to keep the planet from swimming too far away. But there is not much sense, really, in these concatenations. Milton was a great artist in language; he, too, won a victory over the English tongue, but I do not know that he greatly enriched it, and I have felt many times in reading *Paradise Lost* and *Samson Agonistes* that he all but killed it. We cannot advance along the road into which he forced it; and if we wish to learn some of the secrets of creative style, secrets that may be valuable to us now for the production of literature in our time, it is to Shakespeare that we must go. I suppose there are few young writers who have not at one time or another fallen completely under the Miltonic spell; not one of them, of course, has so penetrated into the process of the Miltonic style as Keats, no one else has written a *Hyperion*, though many have tried to write one; but one and all of them, I believe, come at the last to Keats's conclusion: 'The *Paradise Lost*, though so fine in itself, is a corruption of our language. It should be kept as it is, unique, a curiosity, a beautiful and grand curiosity, the most remarkable production of the world. I have but lately stood on my guard against Milton. Life to him would be death to me.' If there is death in Milton, there is life in Shakespeare. The spell he exerts upon us is not the spell of a manner, even though it is a great manner, but the spell of the most richly gifted and the most living of all writers: penetrate into Milton, we shall only produce Miltonics, penetrate into Shakespeare—as far and as diligently as we can—we shall not produce imitation Shakespeare; we shall merely write whatever we are writing—novels, essays, poetry—with a far keener sense of the resources of our art.

I apologize for the inconsequence of the digression, and I ask that it may be excused by the fact that I, personally, find it impossible to regard this problem of style for long without being compelled to relate it to the practice and possibilities of the present time; and inevitably I find myself more or less out of sympathy, or rather out of living contact, with styles that seem to me remote from our present necessities. With the best will in the world, I cannot save myself from being drawn to regard the problem of style as a practical problem. By admitting my bias, I know that I do not abolish it; but I hope that I shall thus be forgiven for the obvious disproportions in my treatment of the subject. I have, for instance, harped upon this process which I have called crystallization, partly because I believe it to be in fact the most important of the processes at work in good writing, but more because I think that to have it definitely before one's mind is actively helpful. If I have emphasized it unduly, it is because I believe it is unduly neglected, and, when it is emphasized, is emphasized in a distorted and misleading way. Just as the rage of the previous generation for 'plasticity' has ended in a kind of descriptive writing which is the absolute negation of style (as I have tried to show in the case of Mr. Arnold Bennett), so today there is a school of poets and prose-writers, engaged in the pursuit of the image for its own sake, a pursuit that can only end in the artificialities of a new Euphuism. The image is only a means; it is an instrument by which precision of emotional effect is obtained; if it does not help to attain precision, if it is not kept subordinate to the whole intended effect, then it is simply distracting and jarring: instead of concentrating, it confuses.

But, you may say, how far does this conception of style actually cover the facts? In her book of *Recollections* which appeared shortly before her death, Mrs. Humphry Ward told the story how, in the enthusiasm of her youthful scepticism, she one day said to Walter Pater that orthodox religion could not hold out much longer against the assaults of science on the one hand and literature on the other. To her surprise Pater shook his head, and said: 'No, I don't think so: and we don't altogether agree. You think it's all plain. But I can't. There are such mysterious things. Take that saying: "Come unto me, all ye that are weary and heavy-laden." How can you explain that? There is a mystery in it—a something supernatural.' Pater's question was not addressed to the literary critic;

but, none the less, it is one the literary critic must try to
answer in his fashion. How far does the conception of
style which has been developed here cover the language
of the Authorized Version of the English Bible, of which
the sentence that haunted Pater is assuredly one of the
most beautiful?

I will try to redeem the incompleteness of my exposition in this and other respects in my next and final lecture; I prefer to devote the remainder of this one to an
elucidation of a phrase which I used a little while ago.
I said that a great work of literature was not so much a
triumph of language, as a victory over language. The
writer is perpetually trying to make language carry more
than it will bear, incessantly doing a kind of exquisite
violence to speech. His actual motive for doing so is his
impulse to find a precise expression for his content; he is
engaged in a purely personal warfare; but his victory,
if he obtains a victory, is not a victory of language, indeed, but a victory for language. Just as a doctor, when
his patient is at death's door, does violence to his body
by administering some potent drug, and thus enables the
healthy elements in the body to gain the victory over the
destructive organisms, so the creative writer injects a
vast quantity of vivid and fresh perceptions into the body
of language, so that it becomes youthful and vigorous
once more, able in future to adapt itself to more experiences and more diverse contents.

On the other side, language itself, as the medium of
communications between the members of a huge society
of people, constantly tends, like the money we pass from
hand to hand, to become defaced and smooth. And this
process is vastly accelerated by the growth of newspapers.
The people who write newspapers, if they have the will,
have not the time to keep their language in trim and precise; if they had, moreover, and used it for this purpose
they would quickly lose their positions. Their business

is to address the average mind, and to do this they must use the vocabulary of the average mind: if they do not, they will be paid the compliment of being declared unreadable, which, when it comes to the ears of their proprietor, will be a sentence of death upon themselves. But without this modern complication, the process of smoothing the coinage of language is natural, and, in a way, healthy. Even if we conceive an imaginary society composed of the most correct as well as the most creative writers, we can see that a felicitous epithet, or a good metaphor, in so far as it is approved by a number of the members, is liable to become current. A new power of definition has been added to speech; it obviously behoves those who can, to use it: and, just as obviously, in use it must lose little by little its precision. It was originally made to express one personal perception: now it has to conform to many. Language at any moment is full of metaphors in all stages of the progress from full vigour through half-life to the moribundity of the cliché; I have not the *Oxford Dictionary* within reach, but I imagine that when Shakespeare made Enobarbus say of Cleopatra, 'But for her person, It beggared all description', the phrase was a new coinage, as bright as it was singularly appropriate to his rehearsal of the gorgeousness of her procession on the Nile. His description of the pageant had been royally lavish: now he was beggared of his resources. But that precision has by now been completely worn from the phrase.

It is the business of the correct writer to withstand this degeneration of language: he differs from the creative writer who is continually making new coinages—not of words, or seldom of words, but of phrases which have the unity of words—in that he has not a great store of sensuous perceptions wherewith to enrich language: but he has sufficient sensibility to appreciate the quality of these perceptions in the work of the creative writer. He needs some one else to make the revelation to him, but he is able to take advantage of it when it is made. And this, as I see it, is one of the chief functions of the secondary writer; though he cannot give new life to language, he can keep it alive. For this task he needs a true and a rich scholarship, of the intimate kind. And after all, it is no small thing to be a secondary writer: he will march to immortality behind Lamb and Landor and Stevenson: he cannot reasonably ask for more.

This is the sense in which I meant the words: 'If there is death in Milton, there is life in Shakespeare.' In Milton there are comparatively few, in Shakespeare there are many expressed sensuous perceptions, of which use has never been made since his day. Many, I know, have passed into the common language; but the vast majority have not. There are times when it seems that no one reads Shakespeare any more; if they go to him seriously, they go to find something he has not got—a philosophy; per-haps they go to find a dramatist, which of course he is; but it seems to me that uncommonly few go to find the most delicate artist in language that has even been. Per-haps some day we shall have a really sensitive study of Shakespeare's use of metaphor, where the author will compare metaphors that describe kindred perceptions. He might, for instance, take the two lines of Camillo in *The Winter's Tale*, as he watches Florizel and Perdita together.

> He tells her something
> That makes her blood look out. Good sooth, she is
> The queen of curds and cream.[1]

'Blood look out' for 'blush'—that is all it is. Yet it gives an almost unearthly purity, and an almost unearthly reality, to Perdita's physical being. It hardly needs to be

[1] iv. iii. 159.

E

told that she is the 'Queen of curds and cream' : we know it. Side by side with this exquisite metaphor, we may put Shakespeare's experiment with it a few lines before, in the same scene of the same play, when he makes Perdita say to Florizel

> Your praises are too large : but that your youth,
> And the true blood which fairly peeps through it,
> Do plainly give you out an unstained shepherd . . .

Between them both might be set Antony's promise to Cleopatra of the entertainment he will give his noble captains :

> and tonight I'll force
> The wine peep through their scars.

Then, again, in *The Winter's Tale*—how characteristic of the play is this delicate obsession with the image!— we have 'Flora peering in April's front'. And, to track this one perception down to its origin, we might compare the phrases in his poems, Lucrece 'who o'er the white sheet papers her whiter chin' and Adonis who

> did raise his chin
> Like a dive-dapper peering through a wave,
> Who, being look'd on, ducks as quickly in.

This is not the occasion to discuss the subtle nuances of difference between these uses of a single image; but they all happen to be examples of that stored-up richness of expression that still awaits a user. To be saturated in expressions of this kind, is to have a language sensitive to the slightest finger-touch, and at a time like the present when the fashion is to insist on the infinite complexity of the modern consciousness, and to make fritters of English in the attempt to communicate this complexity, an intimate knowledge of Shakespeare seems doubly advisable. I cannot believe that its place is adequately supplied by an intimate knowledge of Henry James.

I am not suggesting a course of plagiarism from Shakespeare; I merely suggest that there is no one from whom an English writer can learn so much of the vital processes of style. From Shakespeare he can learn in what ways the discrimination of sense-perception is the most active principle at work in refining language, and he can see to what a point of suppleness the stubborn elements of speech can be compelled by the unrelaxing pressure of an overflowing sensuous memory. Studying Shakespeare is studying how to write. Not that we shall ever write a line like Shakespeare, or, I hope, ever try to; but in proportion as our understanding of the perceptual element of his language becomes more intimate, our own power to discriminate in the sensuous world will become keener. It is unlikely that we shall naturally have the power to accumulate the direct perceptions which reshape and refurbish language—that is the privilege of the highest literary genius; but it is not improbable that some of us possess a little fragment of that power in embryo; if we have, it will expand and become conscious of itself as we watch it at work in Shakespeare. The act of recognizing his perceptions is in itself perceptive, and the delight of ratifying his language, by reference to the reality upon which he shaped it, is almost a creation.

I know of no other sense in which we can speak of style being learned, and my recommendation is perhaps only another version of Stevenson's 'sedulous ape'. Odd and ambitious as it may sound—and in this respect I have the temerity to feel that I am right, and Stevenson wrong—the only writer to whom we may safely play the 'sedulous ape' is the greatest of them all. He must be a Colossus, for our business is 'to walk under his huge legs and peep about'; if he is less than a Colossus, we may be, we inevitably shall be, tempted to imitate the superficial idiosyncrasy of his style. An idiosyncrasy of style is absolutely inimitable; it is the garment which fits, or rather the actual skin which covers a fabric of living nerves and tissue, a whole individual mode of seeing, feeling, thinking; it is no more possible to imitate a real style than it is to be another man. By attempting it we shall not only land ourselves in the mire of unconscious pastiche, but we shall have acquired a dangerous trick of falsifying our own feeling and thought. We are likely to have difficulty enough in getting rid of the mannerisms which are —one may almost say—in the air we breathe, the accepted clichés of thought and feeling and language of the age in which we live, without burdening ourselves with a mannerism we have deliberately acquired.

But Shakespeare is so big and inexhaustible, his idiosyncrasy so Protean, that we are spared temptation. Coleridge tells us that he tried to imitate Shakespeare, and it came out Massinger. But then, you may say, Keats tried to imitate Milton, and it came out *Hyperion*. If you are a Keats, that is, if you have a richness of perception and an original genius comparable with Shakespeare's own, then, of course, you may do anything; you may quite safely imitate Homer and Dante as well. Nothing can stop such a teeming mind from discharging itself. But after all, Keats abandoned *Hyperion* because the Miltonic manner was false for him, because to imitate Milton even with a richer genius than Milton's own is to imitate a superficial idiosyncrasy. I open *Paradise Lost* at hazard:

> He soon
> Saw within ken a glorious angel stand,
> The same whom John saw also in the sun:
> His back was turned, but not his brightness hid;
> Of beaming sunny rays, a golden tiar
> Circled his head, nor less his locks behind
> Illustrious on his shoulders fledge with wings
> Lay waving round: on some great charge employed
> He seemed, or fixed in cogitation deep.
> Glad was the spirit impure, as now in hope

To find who might direct his wandering flight
To Paradise, the happy seat of man,
His journey's end and our beginning woe.
But first he casts to change his proper shape,
Which else might work him danger or delay :
And now a stripling cherub he appears,
Not of the prime, yet such as in his face
Youth smiled celestial, and to every limb
Suitable grace diffused, so well he feigned;
Under a coronet his flowing hair
In curls on either cheek played, wings he wore
Of many a coloured plume sprinkled with gold,
His habit fit for speed succinct, and held
Before his decent steps a silver wand.[1]

It is magnificent; but is it English? There is no reason why it should be; the principal thing is that it should be magnificent. But Keats spoke on behalf of the genius of the English language when he rejected those inversions; those 'but nots', 'nor less' es, those 'succincts' and 'decents'; and, above all, when he rejected those rhythms. 'It is the verse of art', said Keats. He meant it petulantly; that it is the verse of art is the great title to fame of *Paradise Lost*. But art of this kind is outside the main stream of English.

I take the *sortes Shakesperianae*. It is not really fair to Milton, for my Shakespeare has a trick of opening at favourite places, whereas my Milton has still something of the stubbornness the binder gave it. It opens at *Troilus and Cressida* : Ulysses speaks :

Time hath, my lord, a wallet at his back
Wherein he puts alms for oblivion—
A great-siz'd monster of ingratitudes :
Those scraps are good deeds past : which are devour'd
As fast as they are made, forgot so soon
As done : perseverence, dear my lord,
Keeps honour bright : to have done, is to hang

[1] *Paradise Lost*, iii. 621.

Quite out of fashion, like a rusty mail
In monumental mockery. Take the instant way :
For honour travels in a strait so narrow
Where one but goes abreast : keep, then, the path;
For emulation hath a thousand sons
That one by one pursue : if you give way,
Or hedge aside from the direct forthright,
Like to an enter'd tide, they all rush by
And leave you hindmost :
Or, like a gallant horse fall'n in first rank,
Lie there for pavement to the abject rear,
O'errun and trampled on : then what they do in present,
Though less than yours in past, must o'ertop yours.
For time is like a fashionable host
That slightly shakes his parting guest by the hand,
And with his arms outstretch'd, as he would fly,
Grasps in the comer : welcome ever smiles,
And farewell goes out sighing. O! let not virtue seek
Remuneration for the thing it was;
For beauty, wit,
High birth, vigour of bone, desert in service
Live, friendship, charity, are subjects all
To envious and calumniating time.[1]

Count the metaphors in the passage. There must be at least a dozen, intertwined with each other, and inextricable; but not for an instant is there confusion. There are two absolutely new words, invented by Shakespeare for this occasion, 'hedge aside' and 'forthright'. One has passed into the language; the other is only waiting to be used again. 'Monumental', also, in the sense, is Shakespeare's coinage. The perceptual element is restored to it, just as when Othello says of Desdemona's skin that it was 'smooth as monumental alabaster'. Compare Milton's 'succinct' and 'decent' with these!

The only thing to be done with such a passage is to take it phrase by phrase, almost word by word, which would

[1] *Troilus and Cressida*, iii. iii, 144.

exhaust the reader's patience. But whether to call it art, I do not know. Language recharged with native vitality to this extent is a miracle; and I suppose there are some people who would say it was overcharged. But the strange thing is that this evident and irrefutable miracle is somehow perfectly natural; as natural as the waking of a demigod from sleep. Then, I suppose, we feel that all things are possible, and we feel it as we feel the warmth of the sun, with a quiet and unastonished confidence.

If we are writers, or engaged in trying to be writers, we feel after a draught of such wine as that, that our eyes, our mind, our very fingers are sensitive in new ways: we have seen the divinity born out of the sea-foam, and instead of being blinded for our rashness, we are gifted with a second sight. If only we could retain that gift! Who knows but that we may: 'Perseverance, dear my lord.'

Think back to the splendours of the Milton; perhaps we may imagine that we now understand what he meant when he wrote of Shakespeare:

> Whilst to the shame of slow-endeavouring art
> Thy easy numbers flow, and that each heart
> Hath from the leaves of thy unvalued book
> Those Delphic lines with deep impression took;
> Then thou, our fancy of itself bereaving,
> *Dost make us marble with too much conceiving.*

Milton lived too close to Shakespeare. I think that there is a story to be told of what pains he had to take to keep the Shakespearean echoes which rang in his head from appearing on his paper.[1] But we are out of danger, in time and in genius: there is no danger of our becoming marble. We have, instead, the opportunity of becoming flesh and blood.

[1] See note.

VI

THE ENGLISH BIBLE; AND THE GRAND STYLE

I must make this lecture an *omnium gatherum*; a place in which I try to pick up and knot together as many loose ends as I can. I feel that they are scattered everywhere, waving about forlornly.

Instinctively, in an inquiry of this kind, we emphasize those elements which are of most present importance to ourselves; I know that I have done so, and that there is very little chance of redressing the balance now. But I will do my best to be a little more definite about various matters I have on my conscience.

I feel that my assimilation of prose and poetry may have seemed rather arbitrary. If, however, I had made plain my attitude and the reason for it, I should have been forced to anticipate my argument. Therefore, I contented myself with asserting that, regarded as processes of literary creation, the production of prose was not to be distinguished from the production of poetry. Perhaps it is possible to add something to that bare statement now.

Rhythm and metre, which are the formal distinguishing marks of poetry, have the power of throwing the reader into a state of heightened susceptibility to emotional suggestion. Why they have this power would be a long, and perhaps mainly a physiological story. But the plain psychological fact is that the recurrence of a regular rhythmical beat has an almost hypnotic effect; it completely detaches our attention from the world of everyday, lulls the practical alertness which that world demands, and if it is regular and monotonous enough, actually sends us to sleep. That is the extreme effect of

metre and rhythm. The poet's business is to take advantage of the tendency, and instead of letting it reach its
proper physical conclusion, by an infinite rhythmical
variation on the metrical basis, to keep us intensely aware.
There is a background of metrical sameness, separating
us like a curtain from the practical world; there is a richness of rhythmical variation to make the world in which
we are, worthy of our most delighted attention.

In this condition we are amenable to the suggestion
of emotions and thoughts which, on the plane of prose,
could only pierce our consciousness if they had the weight
of much relevant circumstance behind them. The writer
of prose has to take us by slow degrees into an imaginary
world where his suggestions can work as powerfully upon
us. This does not mean that poetry is easier to write than
prose: the difficulty of the prose writer's process of ac-
cumulating circumstance is not a whit greater than that
of the poet's process: the writer of verse always runs the
danger of simply sending you to sleep, or at least of putting all the faculties of consciousness in abeyance. Great
poets have not always escaped the danger. The essential
difference between the two methods is that the method
of poetry when it is successful is much quicker than the
method of prose when it is successful. The method of
poetry is the instrument of a greater and more rapid
concentration. It can take advantage of your condition
of susceptibility and act more swiftly. But a different
degree of rapidity in action is not really a different kind
of action.

And of course there is a great deal of prose which, consciously or unconsciously, adopts the poetic method. The
background of metrical sameness is not quite so regular;
on the other hand, the possibilities of rhythmical variation
are not so great, simply because the sameness is deficient.
Hence arise the peculiar dangers of poetic prose; in which
it is much more difficult than in poetry to make the

rhythmical variations really perceptible. Milton's *Areo-pagitica* is a singular instance, and a singular triumph, of poetic prose. The condition of emotional susceptibility into which one is plunged by it is extraordinary. I am, indeed, inclined to believe that it defeats its own ends. At all events, whenever I read it, the last thing I find myself thinking about, whether during the process or at the end, is the liberty of unlicensed printing. It might much rather be a poem on the immortality of the soul. 'They who to States and Governors of the Common-wealth direct their speech, High Court of Parliament . . .' It is irresistible.

'For this is not the liberty which we can hope, that no grievance ever should arise in the Commonwealth, that let no man in this World expect; but when complaints are freely heard, deeply considered, and speedily reformed, then is the utmost bound of civil liberty attained, that wise men look for. To which if I now manifest by the very sound of this which I shall utter, that we are already in good part arrived, and yet from such a steep disadvantage of tyranny and super-stition grounded into our principles as was beyond the man-hood of a Roman recovery, it will be attributed first, as is most due, to the strong assistance of God our deliverer, next to your faithful guidance and undaunted wisdom, Lords and Commons of England.'

The superb music is too dominant. The only debate that could really be conducted to such an accompaniment is a debate of archangels: and that is what the *Areo-pagitica* really is. One weeps tears of joy at the sheer beauty of the orchestration. But that is not the mood to appreciate a piece of political pleading.

The distinction we can make between prose and poetry is reduced to this: that poetry makes use of metre and rhythm as a primary means of bringing us to a condition of susceptibility to emotion and thought. The employ-ment of this means has an influence on the methods used to communicate emotion and thought, because it presupposes a swiftness of response which the writer of prose cannot assume. A poet may crowd image upon image in a way that will be illegitimate in prose, where if the working of the reader's mind is slower it is also more thorough. But the difference between the two is not an essential difference; it is a difference of tempo rather than structure, except, perhaps, in the case of that prose whose appeal is made directly to the rational faculty, the prose which asks you to compare and to judge.

I do not think, therefore, that there is any improper simplification in regarding the work of literature as the communication of individual thought and feeling, or in taking Stendhal's definition, interpreted largely, as one which holds good of style of every kind, in so far as it is excellent in its kind. I need not return to the question of the comprehensiveness of the mode of thought or feeling, on which depends the greatness of the style; nor to that process of 'crystallization' which is the most vital and most general of the methods of creation. But the distinction I have drawn between poetry and prose suggests some further inquiry into the part played by the reader's condition of susceptibility.

If we regard writing as the establishment of a relation between the author and his audience, it is clear that the amount of compulsive virtue he has to put into his language will depend upon the extent to which the feelings and thoughts he wishes to communicate are familiar or strange to his reader. Where his emotion is particular, his thought and feeling inseparably associated with circumstances that are unique, where his whole system of convictions is individual and in a sense even incommensurable, there he has practically to compel us to think and feel as he wills. He has to put something before us to which we must react in a certain way or not at all, and just in so far as those reactions are remote from our habitual method of thinking or feeling, his task will be more difficult, and his style will need to be more concrete. Not that this will be an alien effort to him. Writers have enough common humanity to ensure that they themselves will feel the necessity of employing their most impassioned exactness to express thoughts and feelings that are remote from the common experience. If they do not feel this necessity, then they are either mystics or madmen, and we have only to regret that the norm of the common experience is sometimes pitched so low, that when a man *has* made the effort he is still reckoned as mad. Two truly gifted minor poets—Christopher Smart and John Clare—were put into asylums, so far as I discover, mainly because of their genius.

But there are certain realms of experience in which the level of emotional susceptibility of the audience is much higher than in others. There is, for instance, the realm of religion. Any deeply religious man is habituated to thoughts and feelings of a kind utterly remote from those which are the accompaniment of his practical life. A man who really believes in a just and omnipotent, a merciful and omniscient God has for his familiar companion a conception and an emotion which are truly tremendous. No suggestion of the poet or the prose-writer can possibly surpass them in force or vehemence. When an old Hebrew prophet wrote: 'And the Lord said', he had done everything. The phrase is overwhelming. Nothing in *Paradise Lost* can compare with it.

> When the most High
> Eternal Father from his secret cloud,
> Amidst in thunder uttered thus his voice[1]

is almost trivial by its side. 'And they heard the voice of the Lord God walking in the garden in the cool of the day.' Two thousand years of Christian civilization bend

[1] *Paradise Lost*, x. 31.

our minds to these words; we cannot resist them. Nor can we refuse to them the title of great style. All that we have, as critics of literature, to remember, is that style of this kind is possible only when the appeal is to a habit of feeling and thought peculiar to religion. Possibly that very phrase 'And the Lord said' might seem even ridiculous to one brought up in one of the transcendental religions of the East, just as some of the most poignant verses of the New Testament are said to be grotesque to an educated Mahommedan.

For this reason, I think, we have to be on our guard against the familiar suggestion that the English Bible is as a whole the highest achievement in English prose style. Not that I think this wholly untrue, but the manner in which the verdict is often pronounced seems to me dangerous. The Bible is a very heterogeneous book. Throughout, the Authorized Version has the high qualities of simplicity and firmness in phrasing. But there is all the difference in the world between the underlying style of Genesis and Job and Matthew. The style of Genesis is possible only to a strict and almost fanatical monotheism; its tremendous simplicity overwhelms us, and I suppose it overwhelms a Jew even more. The style of Job, on the other hand, is that of high and universal poetry. The God of Job is not left to our religious imagination; he expresses himself in language so creative and compulsive that—to use the phrase of Voltaire—if he did not exist, it would be necessary to invent him. And then, for a third distinct kind, we have the style of the Gospels of the New Testament. In the 27th chapter of Matthew there are two masterly effects—I hardly know whether to call them effects of style. They are contained in two quite simple statements: 'Then all the disciples left Him, and fled'; and the words about Peter, after his third denial, 'And he went out and wept bitterly'. These approach to the condition of 'And the Lord said' in Genesis, in the sense that the emotional suggestion is not in the words themselves; but they differ from those simple evocations of an awful conception of God; the reserves of emotion which Matthew's simple statements liberate in us have been accumulated during the reading of the narrative. The personality and the circumstances of Christ have been given to us: no words, no art could intensify the effect of the sudden, utterly unexpected statement: 'Then all the disciples left Him, and fled'. The situation given, the force of the words is elemental. So, too, nothing more needs to be told us of Peter than that 'he went out and wept bitterly'. We know what he felt; to attempt to describe or define it would only be to take away from that which we know. And all through the Gospel narratives there are these phrases charged with a similar emotional significance. 'My God, my God, why hast thou forsaken me?' is surely the most terrible cry the world has ever heard. Put it back into the Hebrew, the only words of Hebrew most of us know, 'Eli, Eli, lama sabacthani'—its force is hardly less. We know what it means.

And then, again, in yet another kind you have that sentence which I put aside in my last lecture, the sentence of which Walter Pater said: 'There's a mystery in it—a something supernatural.'

Come unto me all ye that labour and are heavy laden, and I will give you rest. Take my yoke upon you, and learn of me; for I am meek and lowly in heart: and ye shall find rest unto your souls. For my yoke is easy and my burden is light.

There the language itself has a surpassing beauty. The movement and sound of the first sentence is exquisite, I have no doubt a thousand times more beautiful than the Greek, which I have forgotten if I ever knew it. But still, but still—would it be so very different in its effect in the Greek? I doubt it. In whatever language that sentence was spoken to you, your depths would be stirred. Our common humanity reaches out after the comfort of the words; all that there is of weariness and disappointment, of suffering and doubt, in all men stretches out for some small share in this love that might have changed the world. Apply your coldest test to it, and it remains great style; and when a man appears who can use it again, perhaps the face of the earth will be changed, for assuredly there is a mystery in the love which finds expression in it.

But there is not much fear that we shall have to take such emotions as these into our modern calculations, nor is there much likelihood of a modern writer's being able to rely upon the religious conceptions and feelings of his audience, nor much probability that those conceptions and feelings will be predominant in himself. In so far as the predisposition to certain kinds of emotional experience plays a part in the style of the English Bible, we may leave it out of our reckoning.

The emotional predisposition of contemporary society is of another and altogether inferior kind; so far from being tempted to rely upon it, the conscientious writer finds himself continually fighting against any tendency to appeal to it. The modern mind is bemused by a cloud of unsubstantial abstractions—democracy, liberty, revolution, honour—none of the people who use these words seems to have the faintest notion what they mean, or any desire that they should mean anything. And these obvious examples are not really the most characteristic; the flabbiness of modern thinking is not really comparable to the sloppiness of modern feeling. I can only pick out a couple of sentences from a perfectly reputable and fairly well-known modern novelist, whose book happened to be at hand. The love-making scene in which the words occur might be rather nauseating if it were not so perfectly ridiculous. The gentleman has addressed the lady as 'You royal creature' twice, and once as 'You

unutterable queen'. To which last she has replied, 'Oh
no! I'm a tiny child'. Now comes my quotation:

> He laid his cheek against her. 'I am your baby and your
> father. Your baby taken home again and reborn. Your father
> to tend you always.'

I admit that is a singularly unpleasant example of
modern sentimentality; but it is only in extreme mani-
festations that one can recognize a tendency of sentiment.
I do not know whether the author actually believed in
the verisimilitude of that conversation, but in any case
he was appealing to the empty emotionalism that is current today. No condition of society is more dangerous to
the writer; it is as though he found himself playing on a
piano whose every key sounded the same note. In the
exasperated endeavour to get some differentiation of response out of it he is tempted to exaggerate, to pound
with a hammer upon those senseless keys. Compulsion of
that kind—and it is the characteristic vice of modern
writing—is utterly different from the compulsion that
the writer has to employ. Every age has its peculiar form
of rhetoric, of course, but I doubt whether there has been
any age in which the temptation was so insistent and
insidious as it is today.

Rhetoric is the opposite of the process which I have
called crystallization. Instead of condensing your emotion
upon the cause, which becomes the symbol; instead of
defining and making concrete your thought, by the aid of
your sensuous perception; you give way to a mere verbal
exaggeration of your feeling or your thought. Instead of
trying to make your expression more precise and true,
you falsify it for the sake of a vague impressiveness. The
result is that you forfeit all power of discrimination; instead of taking your emotion down to a solid and particular basis, which differentiates it permanently, you
raise it up to an infinite power. You try to replace quality

by quantity, and forget that all quantities raised to an infinite power are the same. By pounding on the keys with a hammer you merely break the strings.

To return to our discussion of the style of the English Bible. Putting aside the purity of the vocabulary, which was (I should imagine) deliberately made simpler and purer than the ordinary prose of the time, there is at least as much difference between the underlying styles of the book as there is between Shakespeare and Bunyan and a chap-book. There is high poetry; there is dramatic narrative in its simplest and crudest form; there is religious legend deriving its emotional intensity from a passionate monotheism shared by the audience. And it seems better to distinguish between these than to assimilate them, even at the risk of an apparent irreverence. It is obvious that the emotional susceptibility of the reader will vary with the degree of his belief. One who accepts the cosmogony of Genesis will be more profoundly moved by it than one who believes in evolution and the nebular hypothesis; one who believes in the divinity of Jesus will be more profoundly affected by the gospel narratives than one who does not. And yet I am not quite sure; I think that, on the whole, I prefer to say that the believer will be more deeply affected by each separate page of the Gospel narrative, while the man who approaches it as literature will be more deeply affected by certain pages. 'My God, my God, why hast thou forsaken me?' is far less disturbing to the Christian than to the agnostic.

This brief and inadequate discussion of the style of the Bible at least suggests that a useful cross-section of literature could be obtained by regarding it as determined by the emotional and intellectual predispositions which the audience bring to it. I do not think that this method of approach would carry one so far as the attempt to envisage it from the side of production; but the auxiliary anatomy of style would be useful. I mean that we might begin by regarding as the norm of literary style those simple and overwhelming dramatic effects of which 'He went out and wept bitterly' is so notable an example. Their force is supplied by the previous narrative; we have formed in our mind a picture of the circumstances; we know from his own words the nature of the man who has been denied. If we were to adopt, as one critic has done, the distinction between 'kinetic' and 'potential' language, we might say that the half-dozen words describing Peter are merely 'potential'.

'And the Lord said' is an example of potential speech where the charge comes wholly from the mind of the audience. 'Come unto me all ye that labour' is partly kinetic—the actual beauty of the words has a positive effect—partly potential: the longing to which the appeal is made is universal in mankind. And it might be possible to analyse style by endeavouring to separate the kinetic from the potential elements, though, seeing that these elements are inextricably intertwined, I cannot see that it would be possible to do more than indicate the predominance of one element or another. I suppose that the sentence, 'But the iniquity of oblivion blindly scattereth her poppy', is almost wholly kinetic; that is to say, it completely creates its own emotion. You need no context, and you bring no emotion to it. It is, in the words of M. Bergson, a creative and not merely a liberating cause. But, however far we may carry analysis of this kind, it will not help us much. For the general award, we can only say that, other things being equal, that style in which the kinetic elements preponderate is to be preferred; but since those other things include the comprehensiveness of the author's attitude in an appropriate plot or muthos, to judge style primarily by an analysis of language is almost on a level with judging a man by his clothes.

And this is the principal danger in allowing the dogma **of the** infallibility of the style of the English Bible to go unchallenged. By doing so we allow our attention to be concentrated on the accidents and not the essentials of style. It is difficult to object when we are told—as we very frequently are told—that there are two super-eminent works of literature in English—the Bible and Shakespeare; but I always feel uneasy when I hear it. I suspect that the man who says so does not appreciate Shakespeare as he ought; and that he is not being quite honest about the Bible. The reason why it is difficult to object is that there is a sense in which it is true that the style of the Bible is splendid. The vocabulary on which the translators drew is singularly pure; purer than Shakespeare's vocabulary, by far. But the strength of a vocabulary does not really lie in its purity—and purity is in itself a very arbitrary conception when applied to language—but in its adaptability as an instrument. Think what you could do with Shakespeare's vocabulary as compared with what you could do with the vocabulary of the Bible: no comparison is possible. I can conceive no modern emotion or thought—except perhaps some of the more Hegelian metaphysics—that could not be adequately and super-abundantly expressed in Shakespeare's vocabulary: there are very few that would not be mutilated out of all recognition if they had to pass through the language of the Bible.

And, when we consider style in the larger sense, it seems to me scarcely an exaggeration to say that the style of one half of the English Bible is atrocious. A great part of the historical books of the Old Testament, the gospels in the New, are examples of all that writing should not be; and nothing the translators might have done would have altered this. On the other hand, though the translation of Job that we have is a superb piece of poetry, I am convinced that it is finer in the Hebrew original. All this may, I fear, be thought heresy, perhaps even a painful heresy; but I should not have gone out of my way to

utter it, if I did not feel that the superstitious reverence
for the style of the Authorized Version really stands in
the way of a frank approach to the problem of style. I
shall put my conviction most clearly if I say that the
following proposition must be accepted in any consideration of style: '*The Life of Jesus* by Ernest Renan is, as a
whole, infinitely superior in point of style to the narrative
of the Authorized Version of the Gospels.' The proposition
is really axiomatic. It is clear, from a mere consideration
of the facts of authorship, that to speak of the style of the
Gospels is to say 'the thing that is not'. There are four
styles, if there is a style at all. And the same varnish of
propriety with which the good taste of the English translators has covered them all cannot change their substance.
If we examine this we discover only two elements that
can possibly lay claim to be considered creative literature; the actual words of Christ reported, such as 'Come
unto Me . . .' and 'My God, my God . . .' and the dramatic
effects, such as, 'Then all the disciples forsook him and
fled'. The first do not belong to the Gospels, but to their
author, and the second are really not effects of style at
all. It is not the authors of the Gospels who have given
us the imaginative realization of the character of Jesus
on which these dramatic effects depend. Take away the
words of Jesus which they reproduce and nothing of that
character remains. The written evidence of an honest
police-constable would give us as much. The most elementary conditions of the presence of style are lacking.

Style is organic—not the clothes a man wears, but the
flesh, bone, and blood of his body. Therefore it is really
impossible to consider styles apart from the whole system
of perceptions and feelings and thoughts that animate
them. There is a downright viciousness of language which
is produced by a lazy or inflated thought, or an insensitive-
ness to the true meanings of words, which may be called
'bad style', so long as we remember that correctness of

language is at best merely a negative condition of good style, or better of a positive style. In Leigh Hunt's unduly neglected poem *The Story of Rimini* there are a good many appalling lines, and there is in particular one couplet:

> The two divinest things this world has got,
> A lovely woman in a rural spot.

The concentrated abuse of language in those two rhyme words could not easily be paralleled. But the absence of such vulgarisms—against which, as Coleridge said, a familiarity with the language of the Authorized Version is one of the best safeguards—is not in the least a guarantee of positive style. The most confusing of the many equivocations concealed in the word 'style' is that by which good taste in language is allowed to masquerade as a creative principle. Good taste in language will not carry a writer anywhere. Massinger's taste in language was very fine indeed, but I do not hesitate to say that his style was generally bad. His way of feeling and thinking was not his own; his perceptions were blunted and clumsy. Webster, on the other hand, had not at all a good taste in language —at times it was shocking—but his way of thinking and feeling was individual, and he managed to project it into an expression that was by fits and starts tortuous and blindingly clear: he had positive style.

Purity of language, therefore, is a most unreliable clue to style. But this does not mean that it is always impossible to infer the whole from the part. There are some writers—of whom Shakespeare is the great exemplar— whose wealth of sensuous perception is such that in any piece of the texture of their writing you are bound to come upon some conclusive evidence of a distinct and individual mode of feeling. There will be a revealing image, or an epithet used with a new precision—some token of that process of crystallization which is the typical method of positive style—and these evidences, which may be found in all times and places, are reliable. But they are not always present throughout the texture of a positive style: you may infer from their presence, but you may not infer from their absence. With many great writers the main act of crystallization is done once for all when they have formed their plot, or their argument. All that one can say of them, negatively, is that they do not belong to the great revivifiers of language; their style is not the less real for that. This somewhat obvious truth needs to be kept in mind perhaps less by the critic of English literature than the critic of French. Many English-men look to Racine for qualities similar to those of Shake-speare, and, because they do not find them, conclude that Racine is vastly overrated. He is overrated, of course, by those Frenchmen who put him on a level with Shake-speare; but that does not affect the fact that he is a great writer with a positive style. Read any single page of Racine and (unless you are a very good French scholar) it seems very like a page of any other French dramatist be-fore the Romantic movement. But read a dozen pages of Racine and you feel you are in contact with a perfectly individual mind, engaged in expressing through the acts rather than the words of his characters a passionate attitude towards life; but his language is abstract and frigid, almost diplomatic. The only great French writers who possessed the creative verbal power that is on the whole so persistent in the history of English literature were, first, Victor Hugo, and second, Chateaubriand. Hugo's triumphant line: 'J'ai mis le bonnet rouge sur le vieux dictionnaire'—with all its self-consciousness—might be taken as an index of the difference between French literature and English. English writers have never ceased to play the revolutionary with language, but it has never occurred to them to make a fuss about it.

If we accept the organic character of style, it becomes

rather difficult to extract much valuable meaning from the familiar term, 'the grand style'. If the epithet is conceived as applying to the vocabulary, the distinction is not very important: if it applies to the system of emotions and thoughts that a great writer must have, it is not at all easy to see why Milton's is grander, say, than Mr. Thomas Hardy's. All great writers, or none, have the grand style. That is only another way of saying that the distinction does not convey very much to us. If we try to use the term 'grand style' in Matthew Arnold's sense, and restrict it to poetry which contains 'criticism of life', we find ourselves, as I tried to show, compelled to understand the phrase 'criticism of life' in a very arbitrary sense. It is only by accident that the criticism of life which is contained in all great works of literature finds expression in general statements about life. Pope's *Essay on Man*, on the other hand, is full of them.

Probably there are a good many conflicting ideas tied together in a loose bundle by the words 'the grand style'; sometimes, the emphasis is on the character of the vocabulary—and in that case, if Milton's poetry is in the grand style, Dr. Johnson's prose is also; sometimes, on the nature of the plot or muthos—if superhuman or majestic figures are involved; sometimes, on the expression of general ideas about life. Each of these elements is, in itself, accidental to a true anatomy of style. But there is a certain logical connexion between the first two: if the characters of the plot are superhuman and majestic, it seems more or less necessary that their manner of speech should differ from that of ordinary dramatic poetry by being more dignified, though it is worth while to remember that two of the most triumphant evocations of superhuman beings —of Mephistopheles in *Faust*, and of the Devil in *The Brothers Karamazov*—do not rely upon any particular dignity of speech. Dostoevsky's Devil, you will remember, looked like a decayed gentleman in a shabby frock-coat, and spoke like one. He was certainly not the less impressive for that.

If we approach the grand style from this angle, it appears as a means to dramatic propriety : the poet heightens the speech of his superhuman characters in order that they may appear truly superhuman. In *Hyperion* Keats goes one step farther; he does not profess to reproduce the speech of Thea, as Milton reproduces that of the Deity, but merely to give a human approximation to it :

> Some words she spake
> In solemn tenour and deep organ tone :
> Some mourning words, which in our feeble tongue
> Would come in these like accents; O how frail
> To that large utterance of the early Gods!

The grand style is, I believe, a technical poetic device for a particular end, and is not really an equivalent of the peculiar usage of classical poetry, which draws upon a different vocabulary from that of prose. The vocabulary of English poetry does not differ widely from that of English prose. The poets keep a good many words alive that have passed out of common speech, and there are a few definitely poetic words—though for the most part they are better avoided—and, I believe, a few unpoetic words. (I remember that when I first began to write verses, a poet of some renown warned me that 'legs' could not be mentioned in poetry. I have never been able to decide whether it was a relic of the Victorian social convention, or some profound aesthetic conviction on his part.)

I do not think that in the golden age of English literature the Elizabethan made any particular distinction between the vocabularies of prose and poetry, though my scholarship is not enough to permit me to be dogmatic in the matter. The difference between the two languages was, as I have said, mainly one of tempo. Of course, there was the rant of *Tamburlaine*, that peculiar Elizabethan rhetoric which was natural to Marlowe, and which the rest of them could turn on when they liked. But that was a rhetoric of exaggeration: if you wished to suggest that someone in misery might as well kill herself, this is how you said it:

> When thy poor heart beats with outrageous beating
> Thou canst not strike it thus to make it still.
> Wound it with sighing, girl, kill it with groans;
> Or get some little knife between thy teeth,
> And just against thy heart make thou a hole;
> That all the tears that thy poor eyes let fall
> May run into that sink, and, soaking in,
> Drown the lamenting fool in sea-salt tears.[1]

But Elizabethan rhetoric has nothing to do with 'the grand style'. That is the deliberate invention of Milton, first for the special purposes of his celestial argument, and secondly because he was drawn by his deep classical sympathies towards the notion of a peculiar poetic vocabulary, and perhaps also because he felt the necessity of reacting against the influence of Shakespeare. It is much simpler, and I think more useful, to regard the grand style in English as the style of Milton. It is a true and a great style; the perfect medium of expression for a mode of thought and feeling that are absolutely individual. It is as different from the style of Dante—with which it is sometimes compared—as it is from the style of Donne; in other words, absolutely different.

One great attempt was made to imitate the Miltonic style, by Keats. By instinct he knew that it was foolish to attempt to write Miltonics; he had to feel and think Miltonics; and the surpassing interest of *Hyperion* is that it shows that he could, in a way, think and feel Miltonics better than Milton. But they were not natural to him; he could not maintain himself; he raised the pitch of his

[1] *Titus Andronicus*, iii. ii. 13.

own thought to a level on which it could not operate any more. The reasons why he abandoned the poem were, I believe, two: one was the reason he gave, that the artifice of Miltonic rhythms and inversions went against the grain, the other that he had worked his superhuman argument into a position from which it was impossible to continue. He declared that he wished to devote himself 'to another verse alone'. There is, in the collected fragments of his work, a little passage in blank verse—there are good reasons for believing it to be the last poetry he wrote—which gives us an inkling of what the other verse might have been:

> This living hand, now warm and capable
> Of earnest grasping, would, if it were cold
> And in the icy silence of the tomb,
> So haunt thy days and chill thy dreaming nights
> That thou wouldst wish thine own heart dry of blood
> So in my veins red life might stream again
> And thou be conscience-calmed—see here it is—
> I hold it towards you.

It has nothing of 'the grand style': but it has something of great style; it is simple, sensuous, and passionate.

I believe that 'the grand style' is largely a bogey. There are styles, but no style; there are great styles and there are little ones: there are also non-styles. And, alas, no one can have a great style or a little one for the asking, nor even by taking pains. The best he can do is negative: but the smallest writer can do something to ensure that his individuality is not lost, by trying to make sure that he feels what he thinks he feels;—that he thinks what he thinks he thinks, that his words mean what he thinks they mean. Whether his individuality is worth anything is another matter; but mostly individualities are valuable, because they are rare. Nothing will teach a man to feel distinctly: but probably the best way for him to discover whether he does is to leave himself out of the reckoning. To be impersonal is the best way of achieving personality, and it gives him far less chance of deceiving himself. 'A second promise of genius', wrote Coleridge, 'is the choice of subjects very remote from the private interests and circumstances of the writer himself. At least I have found that where the subject is taken immediately from the author's personal experiences, the excellence of a particular piece of literature is but an equivocal mark, and often a fallacious pledge of genuine literary power.'

NOTES

Page 2. The word Decadence is admirably, though somewhat differently, analysed by the late Remy de Gourmont in the chapter on Mallarmé in *La Culture des Idées*.

Page 23. I originally wrote, and really meant, 'rather less than more deliberately'. But the assumptions underlying that use of 'deliberately' are so great and demand so much immediate explanation, that on re-reading I was compelled to put it the other way, and the wrong way, round.

Pages 24, 25. How little in his critical practice Arnold followed his own critical theory may be easily seen from these two contrasted passages from his essay on Wordsworth (*Essays in Criticism*, vol. ii).

p. 140. Long ago, in speaking of Homer, I said that the noble and profound application of ideas to life is the most essential part of poetic greatness. I said that a great poet receives his distinctive character of superiority from his application, under the conditions immutably fixed by the laws of poetic beauty and poetic truth, from his application, I say, to his subject, whatever it may be, of the ideas

On man, on nature and on human life

which he has acquired for himself. The line quoted is Wordsworth's own; and his superiority arises from his powerful use, in his best pieces, his powerful application to his subjects of ideas 'on man, on nature and on human life'.

p. 153. Wordsworth's poetry is great because of the extraordinary power with which Wordsworth feels the joy offered to us in nature, the joy offered to us in the simple primary affections and duties; and because of the extraordinary power with which, in case after case, he shows us this joy, and renders it so as to make us share it.

How far, on the other hand, his theory could warp his judgement may be seen from his dictum on Shakespeare (*Essays in Criticism*, vol. ii, p. 62): 'Shakespeare is divinely strong, rich and attractive. But the sureness of perfect style Shakespeare himself does not possess.'

Page 25. It is this truth which Mr. Hardy has emphasized by his choice of a title for the volume which contains his finest lyrical poetry, *Moments of Vision*. I am happy to have his endorsement of the theory in a letter which he wrote to me when I first developed it in an article on his 'Collected Poems' (*Aspects of Literature*, p. 121).

Page 28. I do not suggest that there is no meaning in the classification of 'romantic' writers. But the pregnant distinction is not between the Romantic and the Realist, but between the Romantic and the Classical writer. This distinction is of the utmost importance, but it is rather philosophical and ethical than literary. The Classical writer feels himself to be a member of an organized society, a man with duties and restrictions imposed upon him by a moral law which he deeply acknowledges. The Romantic is in rebellion against external law, and just as deeply refuses to acknowledge its sanction. He asserts the rights of his individuality *contra mundum*.

This is one of the fundamental distinctions in 'the mode of experience' to which reference is constantly made in these lectures, but it does not enter into the anatomy of style. Shakespeare, I believe, was essentially a Romantic writer, in spite of his political conservatism. *King Lear* is the greatest of all works of Romantic literature. All great writers since Rousseau have been Romantic. The point to be remembered is that the judgement whether a writer is Romantic or Classical is a moral judgement, undoubtedly necessary to a fundamental criticism, but out of place in a discussion of style. The essence of the matter is admirably expounded from a classical point of view by Irving Babbitt in *The New Laokoon* and *Rousseau and Romanticism*.

Page 80. The word, crystallization, which plays a considerable part in the subsequent argument, was chosen after a good deal of misgiving. I first used 'concretization' (*horrific vocable!*), then rejected it for 'precipitation'. Though I was not aware of it at the time, I have since come to the conclusion that I owe the word to a reminiscence of Stendhal, whose definition of style is the central point of the argument. Readers of that curious book *De l'Amour* will remember the part assigned to a psychological process which he names 'cristallisation'. This process is not the same as, nor even strictly analogous to, the process described in this book, but there are resemblances between them; and I am fairly certain that my choice of the word was an example of unconscious memory.

Page 109. I copy a passage from a review of the Poet Laureate's book on the Prosody of Milton which I wrote at the same time as these lectures (*Athenaeum*, March 26, 1921):

Samson Agonistes is the extreme point of Milton's artistic progress. There his poetic vitality is at its lowest, and his craft at its highest and most elaborate. If you have been reading Milton steadily, you will hardly have observed the increasing desiccation, because your interest in the astonishing technical dexterity will gradually have supplanted your interest in the poetic content. But there is one curious lapse in the last chorus of *Samson* which recalls one with a shock to a sense of the elasticity of the finest English poetry:

> But he, though blind of sight,
> Despised and thought extinguished quite,
> With inward eyes illuminated
> His fiery virtue roused
> From under ashes into sudden flame,
> And as an evening dragon came,
> Assailant on the perched roosts,
> And nests in order ranged
> Of tame villatic fowl; but as an eagle
> His cloudless thunder bolted on their heads.
> So virtue giv'n for lost,
> Depressed, and overthrown, as seemed,
> *Like that self-begott'n bird*
> *In the Arabian woods embost*
> *That no second knows nor third,*
> *And lay erewhile a holocaust,*

From out her ashy womb now teemed
Revives, reflourishes, then vigorous most
When most unactive deemed;
And though her body die, her fame survives,
A secular bird ages of lives.

The four lines I have marked with italics are a manifest disturbance of the stately rhythm of the chorus; the movement of their falling rhythms recalls to the mind a poetic delicacy quite alien to the massive and artificial style of *Samson*. The lines happen to be about a Phoenix. Turn to Shakespeare's marvellous *The Phoenix and the Turtle* :

Let the bird of loudest lay,
On the sole Arabian tree,
Herald sad and trumpet be,
To whose sound chaste wings obey.

The same falling rhythm; the same Phoenix. The conclusion is, to my mind, irresistible that Milton had fallen under the spell of a reminiscence of Shakespeare. The irruption of Shakespeare not only ruins the rhythm of Milton's last chorus, but also illuminates the gulf between the artificial poetry of Milton's final phase and the quintessential poetry of Shakespeare.